THE *Healing* WOUND

AUTHOR **MARKETA DAVIS**

Copyright © 2025 by Marketa Davis
All rights reserved.
No part of this book may be reproduced, stored in a retrieval system, or transmitted in any form or by any means—electronic, mechanical, photocopying, recording, or otherwise—without prior written permission of the publisher, except in the case of brief quotations embodied in critical reviews or articles.
Published by *Writing in Faith*
Printed in the United States of America ISBN: 979-8-9889051-8-9
First Edition, 2025
For permission requests, inquiries, or bulk orders, please contact:
Email: Marketa@marketadavis.com

Disclaimer
This book is a memoir based on true events; however, **certain names, identifying details, and events have been changed or altered to protect the privacy and safety of individuals.** Any resemblance to actual people, living or deceased, is coincidental and unintentional.
The author is not a licensed therapist, counselor, or medical professional. The content herein reflects personal experiences of trauma, abuse, healing, and recovery. It is not intended as a substitute for professional medical, psychological, legal, or spiritual advice. Readers are encouraged to seek qualified professional support if they are experiencing abuse, trauma, or emotional distress.
Due to the sensitive nature of this book, readers should be advised that the content may be triggering for Survivors of sexual abuse, physical abuse, or trauma.

Scripture Permissions
Scripture quotations marked **(KJV)** are from the King James Version. Public Domain.
Scripture quotations marked **(NIV)** are taken from the Holy Bible, New International Version®, NIV®. Copyright © 1973, 1978, 1984, 2011 by Biblica, Inc.® Used by permission. All rights reserved worldwide.

TRIGGER WARNING

The contents of this book may be difficult for some readers.

It includes references to mental, physical, and sexual abuse that may be triggering for survivors.

Please care for yourself as you read.

FOREWORD

By Angela D. Wharton
Author, Speaker, Activist, Advocate Founder,
Phynyx Ministries, Inc.

> *God is within her; she will not fall.*
>
> —**Psalm 46:5**

For years, sexual violence has been prevalent in our communities and, far too often, society has turned a blind eye. No one wanted to hear about it, let alone talk about it. The lesson we tacitly received was that this is something that should never be discussed. Such silence produces a community of Survivors who suffer quietly—afraid to speak up. This is especially tragic because giving voice to the pain is one of the first steps in the healing process.

By the grace of God, I have overcome the pain of sexual violence, psychological abuse, abandonment, depression, suicidal thoughts, and unhealthy relationships—and I have transformed these experiences into the fuel that drives me to change the world.

My beautiful sister Marketa has done this as well. She is on an unrelenting journey of healing, wholeness, and self-love, which she shares in *The Healing Wound*. In these pages, Marketa reveals how she has faced the wounds of her past, found her voice, and chosen to live freely in the life God has ordained for her.

In 2017, Marketa and I met after I posted about Phynyx Ministries, our Sexual Assault Wellness Ministry for women Survivors. She reached out to me and shared about her amazing organization, *The Healing Wound*. During that first conversation, I discovered that we had similar experiences, and I am honored to share that we've been connected ever since.

The Bible reminds us that we are transformed by the renewing of our minds. Marketa has renewed her mind, body, and spirit, empowering her to transition from Survivor to Thriver.

I am proud of Marketa for all she has gracefully overcome, and I am thankful that God has equipped her to be the vessel to birth this powerful book of healing and transformation. I believe it will change the lives of all who read it.

> *"You intended to harm me, but God intended it for good to accomplish what is now being done, the saving of many lives."*
>
> **—Genesis 50:20 (NIV)**

FOREWORD

by Dr. Dana Hunter
Host of the *Love, Lust, or Lies* Podcast
Senior Associate Pastor, Bethel Christian Church

When I first met Marketa, it was through the brave words she spoke on my podcast, *Love, Lust, or Lies*. Although very painful, she shared her story powerfully—with a trembling voice and a steady heart. At that moment, I knew I wasn't just speaking to a survivor, but I was witnessing the emergence of a warrior and a leader.

The Healing Wound is more than a book. It's a reckoning. It's a mirror held up to the darkest corners of silence, shame, and betrayal. It's a light that refuses to be dimmed. Marketa's journey—from a wounded seven-year-old girl to a beautiful, bold woman reclaiming her voice—is one of the most courageous acts of truth-telling that I've encountered. Her words flow from her inner childhood experiences to uncover dark places that have caused so much hurt and pain. Yet, they reach out to every reader who has ever felt broken and whisper: *"You are not alone, and your story matters."*

As her friend, and now lifelong sister, I have watched Marketa rise in such a short period of time—from trauma into purpose. Her strength is quiet but unshakable. Her transparency, coupled with her unyielding faith in God, is her superpower. Her story is a gift to the world.

To those holding this book: prepare to be changed. Marketa's truth will challenge you, comfort you, and ultimately, heal you. I am endlessly proud of her, and I stand beside her with love, admiration, and unwavering support as she continues her journey of healing and recovery.

With all my heart,
Dr. Dana Hunter

PREFACE

This can't be real. I can't believe this happened to me. I'm just a little girl with a powerless body. I want to scream as I lay here, but my voice won't make a sound. His giant hands covered my mouth, and his body smashed heavily into me. My heart was racing fast—I couldn't breathe. He's telling me, "Don't make a sound. Just relax. I love you so much. You are so special to me." My body gave up and became numb, but I still felt the pain. My mind entered another world as if I weren't even on the planet.

I couldn't believe that he was hurting me. I cried, the tears falling down my face one by one. I started counting down while watching the clock on the wall, hoping the time would go by soon. It seemed like hours had passed. The worst nightmare began at the hands of my uncle, whom I trusted and loved. He made me laugh; he gave me so much. Little did I know he would become the big, bad monster. He was grooming me to make my life a living hell and destroy my tiny little soul. I was hopeless. I was lost. I was ashamed. I lived in the world thinking it was my fault. I learned to keep his big secret that I would carry for years, and that caused me pain.

My life felt worthless. I wanted to do anything to make it all go away. I fought many things that tried to destroy me: alcohol and marijuana addiction, selling my body—all to cover up my shame.

One day, I began my healing journey. I never thought I would get to that place. It was a journey of hope and worthiness—a journey to release the secret that I was ashamed of. After the abuse I endured, I never thought I would be free and living.

My name is Marketa, and I beat everything despite the odds. I was misguided and misled as a child, drugged with medication for something I didn't have. I was called names and even was told I was crazy. All of that, and all of those years, were meant to destroy me, but GOD said, "NOT SO!" Whatever was meant to destroy me, He turned for good. I became this strong warrior! I'm powerful. I am no longer powerless. I'm an overcomer with a strong voice that is no longer silent.

This is my story of hope that I will keep on fighting for, as long as I live.

NO MORE SHAME!

I pray my story blesses you.

Marketa Davis

CHAPTER 1

My mom was 28 years old when I was born. She had a fair complexion with sandy brown hair. She often told me that even before I was born, I gave her a lot of trouble.

My mom carried me for almost ten months, and I was a very active baby. I would kick her so hard that most nights she experienced heartburn. She would say, *"Girl, you made my feet so swollen; I could barely walk at times."* She gained more weight with me than she did with my two older sisters.

One night, she began to feel pain. At first, she just laid there, but as the pain increased, she tapped my dad—a tall, brown-skinned man with an Afro who was only 24 years old—on the shoulder and yelled, *"I think I'm in labor!"*

He jumped up, rushed to get dressed, and ran out of the house with my mom to the hospital. She was in labor for two days before I was finally born in October 1980 at Henry Ford Hospital in Detroit, Michigan. I weighed 8 pounds, 7 ounces, and was 20 inches long.

My mom later said it was the hardest labor she had ever experienced, and she felt relieved when it was finally over. She brought me home to our house on the East Side of Detroit.

I am the third child, with two older sisters named Alison and Karla. We are five years apart. My middle sister, Karla, wanted me so badly that my mom let her name me. She chose *Marketa,* spelling it like "market," as in the grocery store.

I was my mom's pretty little Black baby with silky jet-black hair.

When visitors came, they thought I was a living baby doll because she dressed me in pink—her favorite color. My mom and dad also had a German Shepherd named Barretta, who quickly became my protector. She would lay under my bassinet and bark like crazy if anyone came too close. When I started crawling, Barretta would lift me by my diaper and carry me around. My dad would yell at her to put me down, but she would bark back in protest.

Meanwhile, my two sisters constantly fought over who got to hold me. It truly was a joy having me in the house.

I was only two years old when my parents divorced. That marked a big change for my mom as we moved into a townhouse.

My earliest memory comes from my very first day of kindergarten. I was five years old and desperately wanted to take my Curious George monkey with me—the one with the red and white striped sweater. My mom told me I couldn't bring him, and I cried all the way to school.

When I arrived, I stomped down the hallway until a teacher asked me what was wrong. Through my tears, I screamed, *"I want my Curious George!"*

She bent down and told me I was a big girl now, that there would be plenty of toys to play with at school, and that I would have lots of fun.

When we reached the classroom, a tall man stood outside the door.

"Welcome to my class. What's your name?" he asked.

"Marketa," I whispered softly.

As my mom walked me inside, I held her hand tightly, afraid to let go. She kissed my forehead and reassured me, *"It's okay. You're going to love school and your classmates. Mommy will be back to get you."*

Mr. Frank returned to the room and told us to find our names on the tables. I spotted mine next to a little girl named Kathy. She looked at me with the brightest eyes I had ever seen and said, *"Hi, my name is Kathy. What's your name?"*

I told her my name, and just like that, we became friends.

I was so happy to have met Kathy that I talked about her the whole way home from school. I told my mom about how we played with dolls and even had a tea party. When we arrived home, I saw Kathy again—it turned out she lived in the same townhomes, just down the street.

From then on, Kathy was my best friend. We played together all the time, and our moms often walked us to school side by side. Kathy would come over to my house, and we'd play dress-up in the bedroom I shared with my sister Karla. Of course, Karla would yell at us to get out and find somewhere else to play.

As a kid, I was a little daredevil, always tempted to do risky things. By the age of six, I had four missing front teeth because I knocked them out after leaping off a giant slide while pretending it was a rocket ship. I hit the ground so hard that my teeth popped out.

I remember running home crying, with my hands full of blood from holding my mouth. My mom screamed when she saw me and quickly tried to stop the bleeding with ice. When that didn't work, she rushed me to the hospital, where I received ten stitches.

The only good part about losing my teeth was getting to eat my favorite ice cream—Superman. But I hated how my sisters teased me, calling me *"little snag mouth."* That nickname stung, and I never tried that stunt again.

When my sixth birthday arrived, I was beyond excited. My mom planned a big party for me with all my friends and family. The basement was decorated beautifully, filled with giant colorful balloons and streamers hanging from the poles. I even had a purple cake with butterflies.

Music played as everyone laughed and enjoyed themselves. We played *pin the tail on the donkey* and *musical chairs,* filling the room with joy. I remember my Uncle James walking in with a huge bag. He set it down on the table with the other gifts, then picked me up and said, *"Happy birthday to my beautiful niece. You're the big 6 now!"*

CHAPTER 2

It was summer 1991, and I woke up extra early, excited because my summer camp was going to Four Bears Water Park. My sister Karla was still asleep, so I went over to her and nudged her shoulder.

"Guess what? I'm going to the water park today!"

"So what? Get out of my face. I'm trying to sleep," she replied. I thought that was mean.

"Fine, forget you," I said, folding my arms.

I put on my favorite Wonder Woman slippers and went to my mom's room to share my excitement, but she wasn't there.

"Mommy—Mommy, where are you?" I called out. I ran downstairs and found her sitting on the patio. "Hey baby, good morning," she said.

I was happy to see her, but that feeling quickly faded when I heard Uncle James' heavy footsteps walking into the kitchen.

"Good morning," he said.

I just stared at him blankly until my mom said, "Your Uncle James spoke!" "How's my pretty niece?" he asked.

"Okay," I replied, the excitement draining from my spirit.

Why couldn't my mom see the monster with red eyes? I hated being the youngest.

My mom left to go shopping, and my sisters went to their friends' houses, which left me alone with Uncle James. While I was brushing my teeth, he came into the bathroom. I remember it clearly—I dropped my toothbrush on the floor, and my heart raced. He wore an old brown bathrobe that smelled like beer.

"Did you steal my money?" he asked. "No," I said.

He began yelling, grabbing my arm, and pulled me hard, saying he was going to teach me a lesson. He dragged me to the toilet, bent me over, lifted my skirt, and pulled my underwear down. I trembled with fear because I knew what was coming next. He forced himself inside me. I screamed in unbearable pain and tried to move, but he had his hand around the back of my neck. I told him it hurt, but instead of stopping or being gentler, he became more aggressive.

"Stop being a baby," he snarled in a deep, mean voice. "Next time, you won't steal from me," he said while thrusting inside me.

I was devastated because I hadn't stolen from him. I had always been taught not to touch things that didn't belong to me.

After he was finished, I went into the corner of the bathroom, got on my knees with my head down, and cried. I didn't know what hurt more—my body or my heart. I was in so much pain that it hurt to sit down. I hated Uncle James! I hated how he always hurt me! The worst part is that even after being abused, life continued as "normal."

I cleaned myself up so I wouldn't be late to the water park and walked slowly because of the pain. When I arrived at camp, Sister Clara asked me what was wrong. She could see the sadness on my face. I looked up at her and said, "Nothing."

I wanted to tell her what had happened and that I was hurt, but I was ashamed to share my secret. My day was ruined; my happiness and joy were gone, all because I was left alone with that monster. I felt horrible—like I had nobody to talk to and nowhere safe to go. I wished I could find a safe place and never go back home again.

To stay away from home, I began hanging out more. I would get up in the morning and go to my friend's house or anywhere else. I wanted to avoid Uncle James at all costs. I knew I couldn't rely on my family to keep me safe from him, so I took my safety into my own hands. In our house, the rule was simple: as long as I was home before the streetlights turned on, I was in the clear.

I started developing ways to cope. I used to dream of someone coming to rescue me and pretended that my favorite girl group, En Vogue, would save me. Uncle James stripped my world of happiness and comfort. He was a monster who took everything from me.

Some days, I didn't even want to live. I know that's a strong statement, but I didn't want to feel the pain anymore. If dying took it all away, then it seemed better than living through this suffering. No child should ever have to endure constant fear.

Meanwhile, my mom was in her own world— working all the time, being with Johnny, and going to bingo with her friend who lived nearby in the townhomes. She started paying me less attention. The more I tried to show her something was wrong, the more she ignored me.

I wrote in my journal as if I were telling her my story, imagining her reaction. I pictured her kicking the big bad monster, Uncle James, out of our home, then wrapping her arms around me, telling me she was sorry and that he would never hurt me that way again. I used to envision this in great detail and hoped someone would find my journal.

I wished my dad was around more; maybe he would have noticed and rescued me. I was just a little girl who longed for a normal life.

Right before my 11th birthday, as I prepared to enter the fifth grade, I wanted a big party with my friends. But my mom said she didn't have enough money. Instead of a party, she offered ice cream and cake with a few friends over. I created scenarios in my mind about how it could be different.

CHAPTER 3

I was filled with unbearable pain and felt turned inside out. My spirit was crushed by the shame I carried. When you are abused, it changes you into someone you never imagined you would become. I was only 12 years old when I started thinking about ending my life—that was how much I hated myself. I believed it was my fault for letting my Uncle James abuse me. I asked myself repeatedly why I let him do that.

The nightmares returned when I turned 11, and they worsened shortly after Uncle James moved out. I had them a couple of times a week, sometimes moaning and tossing in bed. When I closed my eyes, I thought I saw him standing over me. Sometimes, I stayed up all night staring at my bedroom door. Even after he moved out, I still thought he would open that door and pull me out of bed. My sister Karla shared a room with me, but I don't know if she ever knew. She always seemed to be sound asleep. I would cry, but he would cover my mouth so I wouldn't wake her.

To make matters worse, when my mom talked about him, she referred to him as her "favorite brother." She always put him on a pedestal. I was triggered any time someone brought up his name. The flashbacks would start, and I would see him.

I couldn't get his voice out of my head. My heart would start pounding, and my chest would hurt so much that I thought my body would shut down. The anxiety attacks were even worse. I would burst into tears when no one was around. I played the clarinet, saxophone, and cymbals in the school band, but I became so depressed that I didn't want to play anymore. My favorite was the cymbals; I loved the band, but my mind could no longer focus or function. When Kathy or Margo wanted to play, I would tell them, "Another time." I just wanted to stay away from everyone. Uncle James taught me how to hide things well so no one would ever notice or suspect what was truly happening with me.

By 1993, life had shifted again. I think I was thirteen when I had a crush on my neighbor Randy, who lived down the street. He was cute, skinny, and dark-skinned. When Randy's mom wasn't home, Margo and I would hang out at his house. I remember the red furniture, the white walls, and the smell of mothballs. I hated that smell—my grandmother's house smelled like that in her family room.

We thought it was so cool to just hang out and have fun because Randy had an older brother named Anthony. He was about 17, tall and stocky, with a caramel complexion and hazel eyes. On this particular day, Randy and his brother's friends were there. They had a liquor called Brandy, and one of their friends, named Kevin, came over to me. He looked like a little nerd with his glasses and a big Afro. He was also skinny with a dark complexion. He didn't live in the townhomes; he lived up the block. He was smoking cigarettes and asked if I smoked. I told him no; he said it was cool and walked away. Then Randy came over and said his brother Anthony thought I was cute. I started blushing, then Anthony came over with a drink in his hand for me and asked me to taste it. It smelled awful and tasted strong. I choked after the first sip. Then I tried it again, trying to be cool and fit in. It didn't taste like beer. I started acting silly and goofy, laughing all over the place. The room was spinning.

Anthony told me to go upstairs and lie down for a while, but I wanted to go home. My mom would be home from work soon. Anthony kept insisting I go upstairs. I looked over and saw Margo playing a video game with Kevin. Anthony grabbed my hand and took me upstairs to his room, where the walls were painted blue and covered with Michael Jackson posters. He also had a football trophy on his dresser. The room smelled like old socks.

The waves of dizziness were getting worse. I lay down on his bed and noticed him take off his jersey. He said he was hot, then told me I was cute. My eyes grew wide, and my chest tightened with that same heaviness I had felt with Uncle James.

"What are you doing?" I asked in a shaky, quiet voice.

He unzipped his pants and got on top of me. He was rough, and it hurt, but I just laid there, frozen, until he was done. Is this all I'm good for? I wondered.

Afterward, I got up, still dizzy and now sore. He told me not to tell anyone what we did and said I was his girlfriend now. I went back downstairs and told Margo we needed to leave. I went home, took a shower, and went to bed.

From that day forward, everything about me changed. I became promiscuous. I started sleeping with the boys in the neighborhood, in abandoned homes, or wherever we could find a place. I felt unworthy and believed I was made only for sex. My self-esteem was so low. I became "Ms. Popular of the Townhomes." My mom and sisters had no idea what I was doing.

I was looking for love, and the only way I got attention was by having sex. But this time, I got to say when I wanted to do it. I had the power, not them. I became a totally different Marketa. It wasn't even about the sex. I didn't even really enjoy it—I just enjoyed controlling when I wanted to do it, because Uncle James had taken it from me whenever he wanted.

During this same period, while in middle school, I met a girl named Bianca who was from Southwest Detroit—she lived in Mexican Town. We were both in the seventh grade, so we became good friends and started hanging out together after school.

Depression would still kick in from time to time, but I learned to make myself happy—all I wanted was joy. When we hung out, we would go over to her cousin's house. Her cousin's mom would be at work, so we were pretty much able to do what we wanted. Having no parental supervision was cool. One of her cousins was way older than us; I believe he was about 23. He was cute and had his own place in Detroit, not too far from where I lived.

He approached me, told me his name was Niko, and asked how old I was. I was 13 going on 14.

"I see you and Bianca are friends. You should come to hang out at my place sometimes," he said.

"Cool."

Bianca came to tell us that her mom was coming home soon, and we needed to leave. When I got home, my mom was at work; it was just me and my sisters, and they asked why I was so happy. I couldn't tell them about Bianca's older cousin. I just smiled.

The next morning, I got ready for school and put on a skirt and a cute red blouse. I had my oldest sister do my hair because I loved how pretty she made it. Once I got off the bus for school, I saw Bianca.

"Hey, let's not go to school today," she said.

I thought that this wasn't a good idea. But instead, I gave in and said, "Sure, cool."

Bianca and I walked to Niko's house; he lived upstairs in a two-family flat. His place smelled old, like rust. We sat down on the couch, and he offered us something to drink as music played.

"Let's go to the room," he said.

Oh no, not again, I thought. I knew exactly what he wanted. His bedroom had beaded curtains at his door, and his room was painted red. When we got into his room, we sat down on his bed.

"Bianca told me you like older guys," he said. I never told her that! "Let me show you what older guys like to do."

This time, I pushed back. He tried to get on top of me, but I told him I didn't want to. I knew my promiscuity was my way of getting attention and coping, but I just didn't want to that day. I think it was because he was older. He was cute, but it started to feel creepy.

Halfway through, as he ignored my refusal, I yelled, "Stop!" and added, "I gotta go, I gotta go."

I ran out of the room, my skirt not even fully pulled up, and told Bianca, "Let's go!"

As we walked back to school, I kept thinking about how stupid I was for going over to an older guy's house. When we made it to school, we crept in the back door.

Ms. Holmes, the hall monitor, was standing there in the hallway and sent us to the principal's office. Mrs. Barlow, who had red hair, was mean. She never liked me and regularly called me a "bad child," and I hated it.

"Why are you getting to school late?" "We missed the bus."

"You missed the bus?"

"Yeah," I continued. "We had to walk all the way to school." "So, you two are just getting here at lunchtime?"

Before I could say another word, I looked up and there was my mom. My eyes dropped—I knew I was in trouble.

When my mom saw me, she said she was worried. "Where have you been?"

I couldn't tell her. I was so scared that I made up a random lie and stuck with the story that I missed the bus. I added that a pit bull chased me, so I hid. I was too scared to come out until it finally left, then I was able to walk to school. It was a terrible lie, but my mom could never know the truth. My mama still whooped my butt when we got home and put me on punishment for almost a month.

By this time, the mental abuse at home felt just as heavy as the memories of Uncle James. I always felt like I didn't belong in the world. Behind closed doors, I was put down by everyone, especially my mom. Sometimes, my teachers and my sister's friends didn't like me. I wanted to vanish and fly off to another planet.

I used to cut myself after my mom whooped me. Sometimes she would whoop me for no reason, like if the house wasn't cleaned right or if she thought I was lying, even when I was telling the truth.

By 1993, my pain had shifted again. I was still trying to cope with the triggers. By then, those old nightmares had turned into panic attacks and caused me to lash out at others. I remember one day at school, standing in line—a boy named Eric pinched me on my backside. I kept telling him to stop, but he wouldn't. The next thing I remember was blacking out.

But even through all that darkness, a small light appeared. I finally found a teacher who liked me and wasn't mean to me like the others. She gave me hope in my hopeless world. She made me feel safe, comfortable, and made me feel like I could trust her.

She was my English teacher, Mrs. Sanders. She had pretty hair and spoke with an accent. She told me I was good in her class. One day, she even told me I should be a writer—that felt so good to hear. Sometimes, she would let me eat lunch with her and do extra work around the class for extra credit.

When school was over, I ran onto the bus, happy and excited about the book report I had to do. It was about my dreams and what I wanted to become when I grew up. My sister Karla came over to the table and said, "I'm surprised you're doing your homework early. You usually try to get out of it."

Later, after I got up to take a bath, Karla noticed and said, "You're going to bed kind of early." I knew I was out of character, but I was eager to turn in my report to Mrs. Sanders.

That night, I woke up screaming from a bad dream about my Uncle James. I had a panic attack and couldn't breathe—it felt so crazy. I cried softly to myself. The next day at school, my spirit was low because of the nightmare. When it was time for Mrs. Sanders' class, my mind went blank, and I couldn't focus. She noticed I wasn't myself and asked if I was okay. For once, someone noticed my feelings.

What if I told her what Uncle James did to me? I felt a spark of trust. She made me feel safe and supportive. I began writing in class about what had happened. I finally released the secret. While writing, I felt an immense relief, as the burden of shame I had carried for so long began to lift. I wrote her a two-page letter, put it in an envelope, and sealed it tightly. Once class ended, I handed it to her on my way out. I wondered what she would think. I was nervous, hoping she would believe me.

The next morning, I entered her classroom, but she didn't say anything. I wondered if she had read the secret I confided in her. Feeling shy and still nervous, I didn't know how to bring it up. As I walked out for lunch, she called my name. I looked up slightly, my head down, my throat tight, like there was a frog in it. Here we go.

"I read your letter after school yesterday. I am so sorry. What your uncle did to you was bad, and it was not your fault," she said.

I immediately burst into tears. She hugged me tightly and asked if I had ever told my mom or anyone else.

"No. He always made me promise not to tell the secret, and I kept the promise." "It's time for you to tell your mom."

I stiffened. "I can't." For some reason, I felt I couldn't tell my mom what her brother had done to me.

"Maybe I will talk to your mom. She needs to know so he won't hurt anyone else ever again," Mrs. Sanders said.

I waited and waited for her to tell my mom, but she never did. I felt so hurt because the one time I trusted someone and finally told them, they let me down. She had made me believe she would tell my mom about the secret I had buried for so long. I wondered why she didn't. Did I do something wrong? Maybe she didn't believe me. I felt that familiar shame return, heavier than ever, and even more alone.

At the time, I believed that if she told my mom, they would get him and take him to jail. The Big Monster would finally pay for what he had done. But I was wrong. Losing hope, I retreated into my silent world. From that moment on, I never tried to tell anyone else again. I buried the secret even deeper. I went back to believing I was unlovable. I would tell myself, "I'm just bad," just like everyone said. I felt completely useless. I knew I was running—I could feel it—but I couldn't face the thought of talking about what he did again.

I exploded into tears on the bench outside the school. Bianca came and sat next to me, asking what was wrong. I made up random lies about my dad, saying he wasn't coming to get me when I got home. She reached into her purse and handed me a Kleenex, telling me it would be okay. She comforted me, sharing that her dad lied to her all the time about coming to get her. He was never around after her parents divorced when she was eight. Eventually, she stopped thinking about him and pretended he was dead.

If only she knew the real reason I cried that day on the bench. I wish I could have told my friend; maybe she would have told her mom and helped me.

I thought it was over when Uncle James moved out, but I felt invisible, as if I didn't matter to anyone. From that point on, no one seemed to value or care about me. What hurt most was that the ones I needed love and attention from didn't give it to me.

I started sleeping with different men again. It became my only way to feel powerful. I convinced myself that I was made to be used by boys and men, just as my uncle had used me. It was easy to become promiscuous, always searching for the love and security I didn't have at home.

I was angry inside, so I began fighting with my sisters and the kids at school all the time. Fighting helped me release my anger and made me feel tough, like I could stand up to anyone. I didn't care about anything or anyone I hurt.

They wanted to increase the medication I was taking for my so-called ADHD. I would pretend to take it in the morning, but I hid the pill in my sock when my mom turned her back. I hated how it made me feel like a zombie. Medication was never the real problem.

CHAPTER 4

No matter what I did, no one seemed to understand me. They never asked what was wrong—they just assumed I was a bad child. I showed many emotional signs, such as crying often and acting out in school. When I had nightmares, my mom never asked what was wrong or offered any comfort. I was teased by some kids in school, and some of my teachers didn't want to teach me. I was called the "devil child" and the "bad seed." I was always told I was disruptive in class because I talked too much. My anger became uncontrollable, and sometimes I would hit things, like the wall. The teachers would kick me out of class and tell my mom that if I wasn't on my medication, they couldn't teach me.

One teacher, Ms. Harrison, suggested to my mom that I start seeing a counselor. Her name was Ms. Moore. She was a short, middle-aged Caucasian woman with red hair. Her office had plain white walls decorated with pictures of clouds and a bright orange couch that was extremely comfortable. There was a swan on her desk, and she would sit there during our sessions. The first question she asked me was why I was so angry. I just looked up at her with a blank stare. I told her I didn't want to talk about it, and she said, "You can tell me anything. This is a safe place."

In my mind, I didn't trust her. The last person I trusted with my secret was Mrs. Sanders, and she let me down. I wasn't looking to be hurt again, so I buried the secret deep inside. I just sat there until the clock beeped, and she said the time was up and that she would see me next session. I had to see Ms. Moore once a week during my last hour of class, which was math—a subject I hated. I was happy to miss it, but I didn't want to see Ms. Moore either. It felt dumb and boring to sit there listening to her talk and answer questions that seemed stupid. It seemed like she would ask the same questions over and over, just in different ways.

By the time the summer of 1994 arrived, I was ready for a break from school, therapy, and the constant pressure at home. The summer of 1993 was a hot one! We always visited my grandmother Lilly's house on the Fourth of July. She still lived in the same old brown house on the east side of Detroit, the one where we used to live when I was born. She never moved out of that house. We lived a little farther from her now because we had moved to the west side of Detroit. I tried my best to stay home that day, but my mom wasn't having it. I was upstairs in my room, looking out the window at the neighborhood kids having a water fight.

I quickly ran downstairs, wearing a red shirt with blue stars and a pair of blue jean shorts. My mom yelled as I ran out the door, "We will be leaving soon!" I just kept walking like I didn't hear her.

"I know you heard me!" she yelled again.

"Okay," I said.

I went over to where the kids were having a water fight. They were having so much fun with big buckets, water balloons, and Super Soaker water guns. Randy asked if I was getting wet, but I told him I was going to my grandma's house soon, so I couldn't join in. I just stood there watching them. I hated that I had to go over to Grandma Lilly's house. After a while, I heard my mom calling.

I got back home, and my mom was all dressed up. She wore a white sundress and a white straw hat. I hated it when she wore those big, silly hats. We drove a navy-blue Buick with black leather seats, which I hated in the summertime because they would get hot and burn my legs. She played Anita Baker's "Sweet Love" while I sat in the back singing along with her. She loved her music and would always play it when Johnny was over.

We pulled up at Grandma Lilly's house, and Uncle James was sitting on the porch drinking with his friends and my other uncle, Steve, who was my mom's baby brother. He was short, brown-skinned, stubby, and hilarious. He liked to crack jokes and make people laugh. I was not in a laughing mood once I saw Uncle James. I already didn't want to be there because I knew he would be there. He never missed holidays at my grandma's house.

My anxiety started to kick in, and I felt like I couldn't catch my breath. I sat in the car, trying to regain control, as my mom got out and started talking to my grandma's neighbor, Ms. Johnson. Ms. Johnson was Grandma's best friend—a beautiful lady who looked Asian, with black hair and slanted eyes. My mom looked back at the car and yelled, "Girl, get out of that car! You can't just sit in the car; it's hot!"

I slowly opened the door, and as I got ready to get out, I looked up and froze when I saw Uncle James watching me. My body locked, and my heart started racing. That old fear washed over me, reminding me of the terror I felt as a little girl; his presence would always paralyze me. I was terrified as I got out of the car and walked along the side of my grandma's house, trying to avoid him.

I heard him call my name as he stepped off the porch toward me. My knees buckled, and I felt like I was about to fall, my chest tight with fear. He got closer and closer, then reached out and grabbed me tightly, giving me the longest hug. I tried pulling away, but it seemed like he wouldn't let go.

"Wow, you have gotten big. You've become the most beautiful young lady. I miss the times we used to have together. You gotta keep in touch with your uncle," he said as I finally managed to pull away.

I walked as fast as I could to join everyone else in the back, my heart still racing. I started to feel hopeless, as if my tongue were stuck. I felt like that little girl again, remembering all the times he abused me. No matter what, he somehow retained control over me. I hated being forced to go to my grandma's house. I wished I had a choice to stay home, but my mom wouldn't allow it.

I sat in the backyard on my grandma's swing with my head down. I scanned the yard to see if I could spot my sisters, since they were already there. My sister Alison was standing on the back porch talking to her boyfriend, John, while Karla was playing jump rope with her friend, Tiffany.

There were so many people on my grandma's block and at her house that it seemed like the entire street was filled. My aunts and all of my cousins were there. My grandma was so loved. No one even noticed how sad I was. Everybody was laughing, playing cards, and enjoying the music. My mom and Aunt Michelle were always arguing; it seemed like they could never get along. This time, it was about who could make the best mac and cheese. You could hear Aunt Michelle's booming voice all the way down the street.

My mom marched over to where I was sitting. "Come on, Marketa, let's go," she said. It wasn't even dark outside, but I was glad because I was miserable being there with Uncle James. On the way home, my mom asked me why I didn't want to get out of the car. I just looked at her and lied, saying I didn't want to come because I wanted to stay at home with my friends. Here I was, 13 years old, and I still couldn't tell my mom what had happened to me.

Sometimes, I wondered what she would do if I told her, but I was too scared. She wasn't nurturing. She didn't feel like a mother I could go to. I was afraid of her, so I continued to bury the truth inside.

That's where the anger and rage came from. But deep down, I was afraid of my own anger. I was furious at the abuse I didn't ask for—angry with my mom for not noticing and protecting me, and angry at my sisters for leaving me. When boys or grown men took advantage of me, I carried the blame, even though it wasn't my fault. I learned to comply with people and do whatever they asked me to do. My unexpressed anger was part of my depression. I always felt helpless and hopeless. I thought I deserved everything bad that happened to me.

The shame was eating me up inside, even though it was never mine to carry. It was my uncle's fault. But I still kept it in, and it became part of my identity. Whenever I went to see my counselor, Ms. Moore, I would sit in the chair but not truly be present. I would talk about everything else except my abuse. The shame kept my hurt hidden.

When my Uncle James did those awful things to me, it was like I was losing myself. I became smaller than the secret, and it grew huge—like a giant crushing my soul. My silence shattered into tiny pieces of shame, locked away in small shells I never wanted to open. Even when I got in trouble for being the so-called "big bad bully," it was a part of me I didn't want anyone to uncover. It was always there, keeping me quiet and invisible.

One day, Margo and I were walking down the street on our way to visit her sister at the restaurant where she worked as a cook. We could always go there and eat for free. As we walked, enjoying the warmth of the afternoon, a man drove by and started yelling out his car window, saying, "Look at those sexy girls."

We kept walking until he pulled up alongside us, stopped his car, and asked if we needed a ride. I remember he had an old-school blue car, though I can't recall the exact kind. He was dark-skinned, wore a Kangol hat, and had a big gold chain. He asked us again if we wanted a ride, and we shook our heads and walked even faster.

"I like little girls. If you want to make some money, I'm always around the neighborhood. My name is J Rock. I'm from the other side of the bridge," he said. I was terrified. Margo and I ran the rest of the way to her sister's restaurant. When we got there, we were both breathless and shaking. Margo's sister Mary asked us what was wrong. We told her that a man had approached us in a big blue car and tried to offer us a ride. He looked scary, and he said he could help us make some money.

She immediately called the police and made a report over the phone, but we never heard anything else. I will never forget that day. I already understood what men meant when they talked about making money.

After Margo's sister cooked our food, I couldn't bring myself to eat. I guess I was still shaken up from the man in the blue car. I remember her telling me I could take my food home and finish it later. When her shift ended, we got into her red Jeep, and she took us to Margo's house since my mom wasn't home.

We went to Margo's room, and I sat down on her bed as she went to her closet and pulled out a joint. I recognized it immediately because I had seen my mom and Johnny smoking one before. She lit the joint and asked me to try it, saying she had stolen it from Mary. The smell was so strong—it was like burnt trees. Margo blew smoke into my face and urged me to try it. I put the joint in my mouth and tried to smoke but started choking as my throat burned.

Margo laughed and told me to try again, but to take it slowly, not to puff too fast. I tried again, and this time I didn't puff as quickly, so it was smoother. I remember feeling so high, like clouds were floating in the air. All I could hear was Margo still laughing, and soon I started laughing with her. We both lay back on the bed, and it seemed like the room was spinning. That was my first time smoking pot, but it took my mind off what had happened earlier. My mind was at ease. I knew it was wrong, but I was a lost teenager, just trying to find comfort.

As I was walking home, I heard someone call my name. It was Randy's brother, Anthony.

He asked, "What's wrong with you?" I just started laughing.

"Are you high?" he asked.

"No," I said, but my laughter betrayed me.

"Yes, you are. You better not go home like that. Your mama is going to get you if she sees you like this."

Anthony continued, "You should come inside my house at least until you feel better."

When we got inside, I went straight over to his couch to lie down, where I literally passed out. The room was still spinning like it was when I was at Margo's house. He went into the kitchen and got me a glass of water, but I could barely hold it. Anthony sat next to me on the couch, and I asked where Randy was.

"He's at our cousin's house. Don't worry, he won't be back," he said. He took the glass out of my hand and set it on the table. He started to rub my shoulders, telling me I was one cute mama.

"Can we do what we did the last time?" I just sat there quietly.

I can't remember much, but I remember him laying me back on the couch and going down on me. He had his way with me yet again, even though I kept telling him to stop, crying because I didn't want this. Why was he doing this to me? He was very strong, and I was too weak to make him stop. I froze, still begging him to stop and crying for help.

As he got up, I tried to pull my pants back up, but I felt weak; the room was still spinning, and my head was hurting. He then kneeled over and whispered in my ear that I better not tell anyone. While grabbing my arm tightly, he said he would tell my mom that I was getting high. I got up and slowly walked to the door. He whispered again, reminding me not to tell.

On my way home, I saw Margo and her dad outside catching fireflies.

"Hey, you, are you okay?" Margo asked.

"Yeah, gotta get home. My mom will be home soon," I said.

When I got home, I opened the door, looking for my sister Alison, but she was gone with her boyfriend. I slowly walked upstairs, my legs still numb and my body aching from the fear and pain. I went into the bathroom, took off my clothes, and noticed a bruise on my leg as I pulled down my shorts.

I got into the shower and just sat down, crying. I could feel the cool water running down my face. I kept thinking, What did I do wrong? God, why did you let this happen to me again? I'm sorry if I ever did anything wrong. Why aren't you protecting me? Are you real?

I got up and started to scrub my body, almost as if I could scrub Anthony away. I could still smell his cologne on me. I scrubbed and scrubbed until I couldn't scrub anymore. After I got out of the shower, I went to the mirror and told myself, "I hate you so much. Why did you have to be born?!"

I went into my room and got into my bed, still crying. My mom hadn't come home yet, and I cried myself to sleep.

The next morning, I heard my mom yelling for me to get up. Then, Alison came into the room and said, "Mama said get up." I turned over and said I didn't feel good; my stomach was hurting.

"Tell Mama to please let me lie down. I don't feel too good," I added. "What happened to you? You look like hell," she asked.

I said nothing. I had been with Margo yesterday, and we were wrestling with the boys. I wanted to tell Alison what had happened—that Anthony had raped me—but my head was telling me to speak up, and yet the words wouldn't come out. I was afraid that if she found out, Anthony would tell her I had smoked pot.

Later, Alison went to tell Mama that my stomach was hurting and that I didn't feel good. Soon after, Mama came upstairs and opened the door.

"Girl, what's wrong with you?" she said.

I said my stomach hurt and that I didn't feel too good. She said it was probably from eating all that "dang junk last night." She went and got me some Pepto-Bismol.

"Take this and lie here for a while. Don't think you're getting out of these chores today. You know Saturdays are clean-up days," she added.

I just wanted to lie in bed for the rest of my life and never come out. I was ashamed of what had happened.

By now, it was exactly one month into 1994. That morning, I woke up and went to the bathroom to brush my teeth. I started gagging from the toothpaste in my mouth. I thought it was weird because that had never happened before.

I went downstairs, and my mom was cooking my favorite—blueberry pancakes. She asked if I had brushed my teeth and washed my hands.

"Yes, Mom."

She told me to sit down at the table. "Where are your sisters?"
"They are still upstairs."

Karla came down first just as Mama came out of the kitchen wearing her floral robe and pink scarf. Karla and I looked at each other and smiled—we both hated that flower robe. When Mama brought my plate, I smelled the pancakes and instantly felt sick.

I wondered why—pancakes were my favorite. Karla and Mama wondered why I wasn't eating, but I told them I felt sick and needed to lie down. I wrapped my pancakes and went back to bed. A little later, I remember Kathy knocking at the door to see if I wanted to come outside, but I felt sluggish. I didn't want to do anything but lie down. I told Karla to tell her I was still asleep and would come out later.

Over the next few weeks, it seemed like everything—the smell or taste—made me sick. Even water made me throw up, which was really weird. My sister Alison said something must be wrong.

"Mama needs to take you to the doctor," she said. "I'm gonna tell her when she comes home from work."

I hated doctors. When Mama came home, Alison yelled down the stairs, "Keta is sick. I think you need to take her to the doctor."

"I'm not taking her to the doctor. She probably has a cold. I don't have time," Mama replied.

Later that day, Alison came back into the room, closed the door, and asked if I was having sex. I got quiet, not knowing what to say.

"You can tell me," she said.

I told her about the time Margo and I went to a boy's house from school, a boy named Carl who lived nearby. I said we were just playing around, and he told me to take my clothes off. Then I let him get on top of me. But I was lying, because I didn't want to tell her about that day with Anthony. His words still haunted me—'You better not tell what happened.' All I could think about was what my mom would do if she ever found out.

Alison asked me if I had gotten my period recently. "No, not yet."

"I'm going to take you to the doctor myself," she said. Not long after, she took me to one of those free clinics.

I still remember how lifeless the waiting room felt, with its ugly green walls. The receptionist asked Alison if she was an adult, and she said yes. While we waited, I whispered to Alison that I was scared.

When the nurse opened the door and called my name, I sat there nervously. Alison came with me as the nurse led us to the back. She checked my temperature and blood pressure, but my nerves didn't settle.

Next, she handed me a cup and told me to go into the restroom and pee in it. When I came back out, I gave it to her, and she took me to the examination room. The room was so cold it made me shiver. I sat on the table and asked Alison if she was going to stay in the room with me. She said no, so the nurse, whose name was Jennifer, stayed with me instead.

The doctor asked how long I had been feeling sick. I didn't know. She said she wanted me to lie down so she could take a look down there, but I was scared. I told her no and asked why.

"Calm down, the doctor just wants to examine you," explained Nurse Jennifer. "I promise it won't be long."

It felt uncomfortable and yucky, and my bum got cold. I just wanted her to hurry. When it was over, she finally asked if I had been sexually active. My eyes got big as I said yes. All I could think was, *If my mom finds out, she's going to kill me.*

Then she asked if I knew where babies came from. I said yes, I learned in school. Nurse Jennifer called my sister into the room.

"What's wrong with my sister?" Alison asked. "Your sister is pregnant."

"Oh no."

"Pregnant?" I repeated. "Yes."

I never imagined that I could really be pregnant. I knew where babies came from, but I didn't recognize the signs. I was only thirteen and a half years old—just a kid.

The doctor came over to me and said, "Well, this can happen when you have sex. You're too young to be having sex—it's dangerous." She looked at Alison and said she needed to tell our mom.

I started crying, yelling no. The doctor told me to get dressed. I cried the whole time.

My body was in shock; I couldn't believe it. It all felt unreal.

"I have to tell Mama. What are we gonna do?" Alison said.

On the way home, I begged her to drive extra slow.

When we got home, Mama wasn't there yet. I was about to go upstairs and go to bed early when I heard the door open downstairs. Mama came in, fussing about the house not being clean and the dishes in the sink. I could tell by her voice she was in a bad mood. Right away, I knew it wasn't a good time to tell her anything—it never was.

After a while, when Mama finally calmed down, Alison came to my room. "We have to tell Mama."

"No, no, no," I said.

She asked what I was going to do. I didn't have an answer, so we headed downstairs in silence. It felt as though my feet were stuck, and each step was heavy and slow. When we finally arrived downstairs, Alison immediately started talking.

"Mom, we have something to tell you, and please don't be mad."

"What Marketa do now?" Mom replied. I just stood there quietly, frozen in place.

"Mom, Marketa is pregnant."

I felt a quick slap across my face that almost knocked the wind out of me.

"All I do for you girls around here. I work hard every day, and you go get pregnant out here having—" she said as she started ranting. "Being fast with these little boys, I knew I should have been watching you. Now, who is he?"

I finally found my voice. "Carl—the boy from school, he made me."

She immediately dismissed my words. "He didn't make you do anything; you were just being fast."

I kept repeating that he made me, but she refused to believe it.

Deep down, I knew I couldn't tell her it was Anthony—it wouldn't have made any difference anyway.

She then told me we were going straight to the clinic to get an abortion. "I ain't raising no babies around here. You will get an education," she yelled.

Tears poured down my face. I cried hard because all I wanted was to be hugged and believed. I wanted her to know that I had become pregnant as a result of being raped, something I never asked for. Instead, it became another source of shame I carried around, and now, I was even more buried in it. My heart was broken into pieces.

That night, my mom was flipping through the yellow pages looking for a clinic. I remember her saying we would go first thing the next morning.

I tossed and turned all night, barely sleeping as I dreaded what was about to happen. I was just a kid—of course I was scared. Why couldn't my mom see that? Why did she have to be so mean? All I wanted was for her to hug me and tell me that it was going to be okay. I longed for love and affection. Instead, I felt nothing but blame.

I remember curling up in my bed, praying silently that everything would be all right. I prayed and sometimes thought maybe God would answer my prayers one day. Maybe He would shine some light into the darkness and shame I carried.

The next morning, my mom came into my room, woke me up, and told me to take a shower and get dressed because she had found a clinic. I just sat there in silence until she snapped, "Come on girl, I'm not playing. You shouldn't have gotten into this mess anyway, being a fast-tail little girl."

I got up, crying as I ran my shower. She opened the door and told me not to take too long because we needed to leave soon. I didn't even have time for breakfast. She handed me a banana and said, 'Let's go.'

We got into the car, and the whole ride she just kept repeating, "I can't believe this. You've gotten yourself pregnant. I ain't raising no babies. What are you gonna do with a baby at this age? You gotta go to school—you have a whole life ahead of you."

When we finally pulled up to the abortion clinic, I remember people were standing outside holding signs with crosses and babies on them. My mom told me not to say anything once we got out of the car. One lady, wearing a shirt that said *Sister Mary*, grabbed my mom's arm and said, "Don't do this to your daughter."

"This is my daughter, not yours," my mom said firmly as she held my hand and walked me toward the entrance. She told me that when we went inside, I needed to act like I had some sense; that I had gotten myself into this mess and wanted to be grown. But what I craved more than anything was her love. I was scared, and I couldn't get that affection from my mom.

When we got inside the clinic, we sat down in a crowded lobby while my mom completed the paperwork. The walls were painted black, with gray chairs lined up against them, and the white floors looked dingy and unclean. I remember glancing over at a Mexican girl who was crying, telling her mom she wanted to keep her baby.

My mom went back up to the desk to return the clipboard, then leaned down and told me not to embarrass her and to do everything they told me to do. I sat there in fear, wondering what was going to happen next. My legs began trembling, and I nervously started biting my nails. My mom tapped my hands and told me to stop. She always hated that, believing girls needed to have pretty nails, and that I made mine look ugly when I bit them.

Soon, I heard a lady call my name. I looked up and saw a tall woman with dark hair wearing a white coat. As we walked, I pleaded with my mom not to make me go back there, but she told me to let go. The woman introduced herself as Claudia and took me to a room at the end of the hall. Inside, there was a big black table with long metal pieces at the end—stirrups, as I later learned.

Claudia handed me a gown and told me to go into the bathroom to undress. Out of the corner of my eye, I could see my mom watching me closely.

When I came out of the bathroom, clenching my hands together, Claudia told me to sit on the table until the doctor arrived. Then she turned to my mom and said she couldn't stay during the procedure. My mom questioned why she couldn't remain since I was a minor.

I sat on the cold black table, more nervous than ever, tears streaming down my face. The door opened and closed a few times before a very tall doctor finally entered. He was so tall he reminded me of the Green Giant. He introduced himself as Doctor Aaron.

The nurse glanced at my mom, reminding her of what had been said earlier, and then walked over to me. I begged and pleaded with my mom not to leave, grabbing her hand and trying to pull her back.

The nurse approached and said, "Your mom has to go, sweetie. She will be outside in the lobby waiting for you when we are done."

The door closed behind my mom as she left. Dr. Aaron walked over to the table and told me that what he was about to do would be painful. He instructed me to lie back and began examining me. My anxiety spiked, and it felt like I couldn't catch my breath. My heart started racing, so the nurse came over, grabbed my hand, and told me I had to stay very still.

When it was over, he walked up to me as I cried and said we were done. He told me there was to be no more playing around and that I should get plenty of rest. The experience I had on the other side of that door is something I would not wish on anyone. It is a day I will never forget and one I never want to relive. Was that what an abortion was? Why did my mom make me do that?

The nurse came back to the table and told me I could get dressed. She helped me down, and I felt so sore—my stomach cramped badly, and my legs hurt so much it was difficult to walk. She helped me get dressed, then walked me back to my mom.

I kept my head down, embarrassed and ashamed. My mom went to the front desk, where they gave her a prescription for me because of the intense pain I was in.

When we reached the car, I could barely get in, so my mom had to help me into the back seat. I lay there, still crying, wishing I could crawl into bed, hide, and never come out.

CHAPTER 5

After I got home, my mom told me to go upstairs to lay down. I felt absolutely horrible. I went to the bathroom, and it seemed like I was bleeding endlessly, like a river. Several thoughts raced through my mind: *I hope I don't die. This is scary. Why did I get pregnant? Why didn't I just go home? Why did I go to Anthony's house? Maybe my mom was right. Maybe I was being fast.*

I put on my yellow nightgown and curled up in my bed. I hated the way I felt. My sister Karla came into the room and asked if I was okay. I told her how scary it was and how the painful thing that was put inside me had sounded like a vacuum. I never wanted to do that again. My crying got worse after I spoke; it was like I couldn't stop crying as Karla consoled me.

A little while later, my mom came upstairs to give me my medicine for the pain. Everything just felt unbearable—the hurt, the shame, and even more so the silence inside me. *Why did my life have to be so hard?* I desired to be normal. This was something I could never tell anyone because it felt too embarrassing to say.

For the next week, I stayed hidden inside. I was afraid of seeing Anthony, especially since he lived right down the street. I could never face him again after what he did to me. He destroyed my inner soul just like my Uncle James and the rest did. I could never get back what they took from me. I never felt the same again—in fact, I felt even worse. I felt like I was being punished for keeping secrets.

But even in the middle of all that pain, time didn't stop. Slowly, life kept moving forward, pulling me along whether I was ready or not.

I was 14, nearing the end of middle school with graduation only a few weeks away, and everyone was talking about a party a girl named Jessica was hosting. I knew it was going to be cool—she was the most popular girl in school.

They called her China because she looked like she was mixed with Black and

Chinese. She had silky, long black hair and was big in fashion. She had every pair of colored jeans. During lunch at school one day, she came over and asked me if I wanted to come to her party. At first, I looked around like she couldn't be talking to me.

"You are coming or what?" she asked. "Yes, I will be there."

When I saw my friend Nicole in the hall, I ran up to her and told her I was invited to Jessica's party. We both screamed. I talked about it the rest of the school day, telling all my friends.

After school that day, real life crept back in. I asked Kathy if she wanted to go. She said she had to ask her mom. I had to ask mine too, and I already knew she was going to say no.

My mom was getting ready for work when I got home, and I could smell her favorite perfume in the air. She was sitting on the side of the bed when I walked past her room. Figuring this might be the best moment to ask, I walked to her door and stared at her for a bit.

"Why are you looking like that? Did you get in trouble at school?" she asked while looking up at me.

"No. Can I go to this party Saturday?" I blurted out. "A girl invited me from school." "Girl, you ain't going to no party. You just want to be fast with the fast girls," she said.

Her words stung, but I walked away already plotting. I had to plan how I was going to that party. My momma wasn't stopping me.

I came up with a plan to sneak out when my mom's boyfriend, Johnny, came over. Her attention was always on him. Like always, she loved her some Johnny.

I went into my closet and picked out my Guess mini skirt with my purple blouse. I had to look fly at this party. LJ from my band class was going to be there too. He was tall and cute with wavy hair. I called Kathy to see if she was going to the party, and she said her mom said she could go. Perfect! We were in.

Not long after, I heard the doorbell ring. It was Johnny. Yes! I went downstairs to play it off. My mom was sitting at the table, smoking her cigarette while Johnny was in the kitchen fixing himself some food. He said hello, and my mom got up to turn on the music. They were about to play cards. I heard her ask Johnny what time his brother Ron was coming over.

That was my cue. I went back upstairs into my sister Alison's room and borrowed her big hoop gold earrings; she and Karla were gone. I went into my room and quickly got dressed, then I tiptoed down the stairs one by one. When I got to the middle, I looked to see if I saw my mom. She was sitting in the living room playing cards with Johnny and his brother. The music was still blasting, and no one was paying attention.

With my heart racing, I got to the door at the bottom of the steps, opened it slowly, and slipped out. I ran down the street to Kathy's house. I knocked on her door and said, "Let's go!"

"You're wearing that short skirt?" she asked. "Yes!"

We started walking, excitement buzzing in the air. As we headed to the party, we saw Randy and Carl—they were also on their way. Randy told me I looked cute, and hot with that skirt on. I smiled and said, "Thanks."

When we made it to the party, the music was pumping. It was hype, the disco lights were spinning, and it seemed like China had a house full. I looked up and LJ was standing by the stairs talking to his friend. I asked Kathy if I should say something to him.

"Yes, girl!"

I went over to him, feeling shy. "Hi LJ."

"Hey," he said. "Wow, you look nice."

I was smiling and blushing as I listened to him talk. Then he asked me to dance. I said okay, and we started dancing away. China came over and said, "I see you made it." LJ started looking at her, so I just walked away and went back to where Kathy was.

Trying to play it cool, I wandered over to the food table. That's when I saw China's cousin slip some liquor into the punch. I grabbed a cup, took a sip, and it was good.

After a while of drinking, I felt silly. I went to sit down while Kathy was dancing. I looked up and saw Randy walking towards the front with his brother, Anthony. My eyes got big. My stomach dropped, and panic rushed through me. I hurried over to Kathy.

"We gotta go, we gotta go," I said. "Why?"

"I have to get home. My mom is going to kill me if she finds out I'm at this party." She shrugged me off. "Girl, chill!"

But I couldn't chill. I felt dizzy as Anthony walked over to me. I started shaking with fear and my heart was pounding. He grabbed my arm and whispered in my ear, "You ain't told nobody, right? You better keep that secret." Immediately, I started having flashbacks of him on top of me.

"Let me go, please!"

This boy raped me and got me pregnant. I didn't want to be near him. No one could hear us since the music was loud, and no one was even paying attention. He walked me to the back, holding my arm, and put his hand up my skirt. I pulled away fast and ran out the back door. I left Kathy behind. I was scared and had to get away.

With tears in my eyes, I ran all the way home. When I got to the door, I opened it slowly. The music was still playing and my mom's company was still there. I managed to sneak back into the house, still shaken up from seeing Anthony. I put my nightgown on and lay in my bed.

That night, I cried harder than I had in a long time. I thought about how he still got to walk around like he was that cool boy. He ruined everything. My mom never knew about me sneaking out to that party. I was so lucky because if she would have found out, I would have been in trouble. But even getting away with it didn't change the truth—I was broken inside. And yet, it didn't stop me from sneaking out again.

As time went on, I found myself slipping into habits that helped me escape. When my mom was at work or Johnny was over, those were my chances to sneak out. Margo and I were always doing something; they called us Salt and Pepper.

One of those days became a turning point. Margo and I went to the abandoned house down the street from where her brother lived. It was white and the windows were boarded up, but you could get in through the back. This was the hang-out spot, a safe place where we could chill with no adults around. We did what we wanted to.

Margo invited her friend Jimmy over. He was short and white with freckles and red hair. He brought his nephew Robert, who was also white, kind of tall, and handsome. Jimmy had dice and liquor. It was my first time shooting dice. They called it shooting craps, and Jimmy said whoever lost had to strip.

He asked me if I was down. I hesitated, but deep inside, I wanted to look cool, to belong. I said what the heck. Jimmy explained the rules: if I got a seven, I won; if I rolled a two or three, I lost. I rolled the dice, they hit the floor, and I got a three.

"Dang it!"

"Now show me what you got," Robert said.

I took off one shoe. He said, "That's not it." I gave him a dumb look and took off my shirt. He rolled and got seven—lucky him.

"All right, my turn again!" I thought to myself. *Lucky number seven, come on.* Nope. I got a three for the third time! I had to take my pants off. I got nervous this time, but I showed no fear, even though I felt it on the inside.

We went back and forth. He stripped down to his underwear. I laughed to myself because he was so skinny. Finally, I hit that seven. By then, Robert was standing naked. He was mad, but I walked away with something new—I had learned how to shoot craps, and that day, baby, I won. Game over.

After he put his clothes back on, we sat there drinking liquor. The whole time we laughed and giggled.

But behind the laughter, a pattern was setting in. Drinking became my best friend again. It was my way of coping. I thought I had found a way to numb my pain, but really, I was just burying it deeper.

I hid it so well no one ever knew. That's when I started sneaking liquor. I began stealing my mom's boyfriend Johnny's brandy. Every time he came over, he brought his favorite. Whatever it was, it was fine with me—as long as my mind was at ease.

But even while I was numbing myself, life kept moving forward. It was my first year in high school, in 1995. I was 15 years old and in the ninth grade. I knew mostly everyone from my school because most f them were from the hood I grew up in off Warren Ave. I always had to dress in the latest fashions, and I had a body like a grown woman.

Because of that, I often got hit on by older men. I remember a teacher once told me I was extra nice looking, and I took it as a compliment. I didn't think twice about it.

One day, I was walking to school with my new friend Tina, who had moved into the townhomes. She was Black, kind of tall and skinny, so they called her Toothpick. She was 15, just like me.

As we were walking, I heard loud music. I looked up and saw a green truck riding slowly.

A man leaned out and said, "Hey, where you going?" "School," I said.

"You need a ride?"

"No, we are good," I said with a stern voice. Tina was like, "Girl, let's hurry up."

He asked me if he could get my number. I told him I was 15. He laughed, "You look grown as hell."

I gave him my number, smiling as he said, "My name is Michael. What's yours?" "Keta."

"I'll see you around."

I was geeked. I couldn't believe I had pulled a guy with a big green truck with rims. When we got to school, I told my friend Cindy.

"How does he look?" she asked.

I described him as Black, kind of chubby, and bald-headed with glasses. Then I started talking about his truck.

"Girl, he is a grown man," she said.

I didn't care. I had been through experiences. In my head, I thought I could handle it. I told myself just go with the flow.

When school was over, I couldn't wait to get home. I ran upstairs to my room. Karla was in there on the phone. I was hoping she wouldn't be on long, just in case Michael called—since we had a one-way.

She finally got off the phone, and every time it rang, I thought it was him. Later that evening, he finally called, and I was glad I answered before my mom. I didn't want her to know any of this.

He told me he was older than I thought—he was 27.

"I can do something for you. You look sexy as ever. I can't believe you are only fifteen with that body," he said.

After that, everything started to feel like a secret routine. He began taking me to school. I would meet him at the corner, and he would drop me off. I would sneak to see him, lying to my mom and saying I was going to Margo's or Kathy's.

He started giving me money and buying me shoes. I remember when he bought me some Donna Karan sneakers. I told my mom they were Margo's. The girls at school were jealous. Back then, the money and the attention had me hooked—it felt like I was winning, even though deep down I didn't realize how dangerous it really was.

One night I went out with him and told my mom I was going to the movies with Kathy. I put on the tightest jeans and sneakers, with my rainbow shirt and hoop earrings. I met him on the corner by the church behind our house.

We drove around for a while until we ended up at Belle Isle Park. Once we got there, he parked and turned off the music.

Suddenly, he leaned over and pressed his mouth against mine, tongue kissing me. I froze. I didn't like it—not one bit. Inside, I felt uncomfortable, but on the outside, I didn't know how to react.

He leaned back, his hands sliding up to rub my breasts. "You got some nice ones," he said. Fear rushed through me.

"I said wait."

He stopped for a moment, but then started again, pressing. He kept telling me he wanted me. I already knew what he meant—he wanted sex.

"Let's go to the back seat," he said.

He took off his shirt, pulled my pants down, and got on top of me. I spaced out, my mind somewhere else, as we had sex in his truck.

After it was over, he told me not to tell anybody and handed me money.

"It's gonna be a lot more where this came from. You're my girlfriend now," he said.

When I got home, my mom was in the basement washing. I rushed straight to the bathroom, turned on the water, and showered as fast as I could. I wanted to scrub it all away.

No matter how hard I washed, I couldn't shake the feeling—I felt dirty.

The more we had sex, the more money he gave me. That's how I learned about getting fast money. In my mind, it felt easy—all I had to do was give up my body. That's what I believed I was worth, that's what I thought I was good at.

But the truth was, I never liked the sex. It always reminded me of my uncle. Every time it happened, it wasn't about love—it was about control.

He started taking me to these parties, and he would tell me all I had to do was dance. He would give me a bag of clothes from his back seat so I could look sexy.

One night, we went to this green house with brown wood floors and furniture. His friends were sitting at this big black table. One guy said I was pretty, that my body was nice, and asked Michael if I was his friend.

"Do you want to dance for me?" he asked. I was quiet. He asked again and said, "I got something for you if you do."

Michael turned on the music as his friend leaned towards him. "Dance, move your body around. Let me see what you got," he said. He grabbed my behind and said I had a big one.

So, I danced for these grown men. I had no idea what I was doing, but I quickly learned.

It became a routine. I did it twice a week until Michael wanted me to start doing more. He wanted me to start having sex with them.

One day, we went back to that same ol' green house. When we got there, his friend was waiting at the top of the stairs. He wore black silk PJs.

"Go upstairs with Chris," Michael said.

I went, and he grabbed my hand and took me to his room. He had a black bed that looked like it was a king size. The room was painted gray, and it smelled like burnt trees. On the floor sat a big Tigger stuffed animal.

He picked me up, laid me on the bed, kissed me, and started taking off my clothes.

One day, we went back to that same ol' green house. When we got there, his friend was waiting at the top of the stairs. He wore black silk PJs.

"Go upstairs with Chris," Michael said.

I went, and he grabbed my hand and took me to his room. He had a black bed that looked like it was a king size. The room was painted gray, and it smelled like burnt trees. On the floor sat a big Tigger stuffed animal.

He picked me up, laid me on the bed, kissed me, and started taking off my clothes. He was very rough and had his way with me, forcing things I didn't want—including making me choke when he pushed me to give him a blow job. I didn't want to do it, and all I could think was how much I wanted him to hurry up and be done. While he was on top of me, he said he enjoyed the young ones.

After it was all over, he gave Michael some money. Then he gave me $50 and said,

"That's my girl."

In that moment, I believed it was okay to use my body to get whatever I wanted. I wanted to keep my mind off my past by running from it. I never wanted to stop because escaping made me feel like I had control.

Over time, I formed a new identity. I would turn into someone else, like I wasn't Marketa. In fact, I didn't know who I was anymore. I always believed my uncle when he told me all I was good for was sex. Those words stuck with me all through my teenage years. That's why it was so easy for me to give myself away.

I would drink sometimes right before I had sex. I didn't want my mind to be there—I wanted to block it out.

I remember one day I came into the house, and my sister Karla said she saw me get out of a green truck. I played dumb like I didn't know what she was talking about. She said she saw me when she was walking back from the store.

I told her that was a friend. She asked what friend. I told her me and Tina met him when we were walking to school. She asked how old he was, but I ignored her. When she asked again, I said nineteen. She told me he was too old for me.

I begged her not to tell Mama. Karla was a pretty cool sister; she didn't have a big mouth like Alison. Karla kept the secret and told me not to get caught.

Even with the warning, I continued to see Michael. That's when he became controlling—telling me I had to do whatever he said and that I was going to make more money for him. "If you want to stay in the game," he told me, "you have to do what grown women do." But I wasn't a grown woman. I was a kid. In his mind, though, he didn't see me like that.

Looking back, I realize that was the moment childhood slipped further and further away from me.

CHAPTER 6

"Grown women make money."

I could still hear Michael's voice echoing in my head. "It's all about making these men happy," he would say.

One afternoon, when I was sixteen, those words became more than just something he said. He picked me up from school. I had told my mom I had to stay late, so Tina's mom would bring me home.

When Michael pulled up, I was talking to a boy named Jeremy. He was tall, cute, and all the girls at school liked him. He was the quarterback of the football team.

Michael blew the horn and yelled for me to come on. I quickly walked to the truck, telling Jeremy I would talk to him later.

When I got in, Michael asked who I was talking to. I told him just some boy in school, nothing serious.

Before I could explain further, I felt a quick slap across my face. I didn't even know what hit me.

"I better not see you talking to any of the schoolboys again," he said.

I was in shock. My face was stinging, and a tear rolled down my cheek. I couldn't believe he had hit me. I was frightened because he had never done that before. Then he said I belonged to him—whatever that meant.

The rest of the ride was silent. I just held my head down and didn't say a word the whole way to his house.

When we got inside, he asked if I was hungry. I said just a little, and he ordered pizza.

I sat on the couch, and then he came over, massaging my shoulders and telling me I was his girl, that he wanted me. He laid me down on the couch, pulled my pants down, and performed oral sex on me.

As he pushed harder, the pain made me speak up. "Slow down—you're hurting me," I said. But he didn't care. He just kept at it, ignoring my words. By the time it was over, I was left disgusted.

After he was done with me, Michael told me he had a friend he wanted me to meet and make happy. He explained the job—$60 for a blow job, $90 for intercourse, and $120 for both.

As much as I wanted to turn the job down, I knew Michael wouldn't like it. I was only 16, turning tricks, and my body was tired. I didn't want to do this anymore. I would get bruises on my thighs because the men were rough.

All I wanted was to be normal again—to laugh, to have fun with my friends. I just wanted to feel free. Instead, everything was about sex all the time.

When the pizza came, I just sat there staring at it. I didn't want to eat. I told Michael I needed to go home 'cause my mom was going to be looking for me.

We got into the truck, and he reached over and grabbed my arm, squeezing it tightly. I tried to pull away, but he gripped me harder. "Remember that job I need you to do," he said.

When we pulled up to the corner of my block, I got out. I saw my mom's boyfriend Johnny was over as I walked toward my house. That was a relief for me—it meant she wasn't going to ask any questions.

I opened the front door quietly, sneaking past my mom and

Johnny in the front room. I went straight to my bedroom and sat down on my bed, thinking about this job that Michael wanted me to do—and how I was going to get out of it.

I got up and went into the bathroom to take a shower. As the water ran, I cried, feeling the heavy weight of emotional hurt. I wanted out. That fast money wasn't good money anymore.

About a week passed with no word from Michael. Then he finally called and told me he was in jail. I never asked him why. He said he was coming to pick me up that weekend.

As soon as I hung up, I started thinking again about that job he wanted me to do. I called my friend Tina and told her Michael was back from jail and how he wanted me to do this job with his friend. She started calling me a trick. I was so ashamed of that word and what I had become. Was I really a trick? I just laughed it off and told her to shut up.

Later that day, I needed to escape my thoughts, so I took a cab over to Cindy's house. She had the coolest mom because she would let us drink alcohol.

When I got there, Ms. Wilson was at the brown wooden table. I remember the walls in their dining room were a mint green color. She was smoking a joint and asked me if I wanted to hit it. At first, I told her no, but she insisted, so I puffed a couple of times.

It was strong. I started giggling as usual and thought I saw little silver dots flying around the room. It was crazy, but I was feeling good. Cindy came downstairs, and her mom told her to go get her Crown Royal. When she came back, she poured us some. I sipped a little bit, and it felt like my throat was burning.

Not long after, I heard the doorbell ring. A tall white man wearing glasses walked in. Ms. Wilson said hello to Tim, then he looked straight at Cindy.

When I glanced over at Cindy, she looked like she had seen a ghost. She held her head down the whole time. Tim sat down and played cards with Ms. Wilson, all while staring at Cindy.

I was trying to stay focused, but I still felt high. I remember seeing Ms. Wilson look up and give Tim a look. That's when he got up and grabbed Cindy's hand. She quickly snatched it away.

"She knows what to do. She's gotta help pay the bills around here," her mom said. Cindy and Tim went upstairs, and I remember it seemed like they were gone for a long time.

When Cindy finally came back downstairs, it looked like she had been crying. Then Tim came downstairs, buttoning up his shirt. I went over to Cindy and asked her if she was okay. She said she was fine, but then she ran back upstairs, and I went behind her.

She was in the bathroom, throwing up. I tried to help her, but I still felt kind of high. Afterward, we went into her room, and I kept asking her what had happened.

At first, she hesitated, but then she explained that her mom made her have sex with Tim, just so the bills could be paid. Afterward, she begged me not to tell anyone. I was in total shock, but I promised to keep her secret.

I thought about how I could help her when I couldn't even help myself. I was still keeping my own secret, still struggling to face my reality.

Not long after, Cindy disappeared for two weeks. She wasn't in school, and during that time, I kept thinking about her.

The weekend came, and it was time for Michael to come over. This was the weekend I had to do that job. He pulled up and came into the house for a few minutes since my mom was at work.

We had moved into a two-family flat close to Hamtramck on the northeast side of Detroit, and my sister Karla lived upstairs. That day, Michael gave her what I guessed was hush money. He always had money because he was also a drug dealer on the side.

After a short while, we got in his truck, and he blasted N.W.A. as we smoked a joint. I remember thinking I had to get high so I wouldn't think about the job. Trying to distract me, he told me to look in the back for the new dress he bought me. I reached in the back and pulled out a black dress with lace on it. It was ugly, but I had to wear it.

As time passed, I grew nervous when the truck started slowing down. We pulled up at a red motel, and people were standing outside as I slowly got out of the car, dragging my feet because I didn't want to go in.

I noticed a Black lady wearing a red dress with black heels. She had a nose ring and bright red lipstick. She was yelling, asking what I was doing with that man. "You are too young," she shouted. I guess she knew the game. Michael told her to shut up and mind her business.

Despite my hesitation, we made our way up to the motel room. The hall was so nasty that I wanted to throw up. All you could smell was smoke. The room wasn't clean either. The walls were supposed to be white, but they looked dirty. The carpet was green and old-looking.

Michael handed me that so-called sexy black dress and told me to go to the bathroom to freshen up. As I stepped inside, I saw a roach running across the floor. I wanted to run back out of there.

Forcing myself to continue, I came out, and Michael walked over to me, rubbed my arms, and told me I looked good.

"Do I have to do this?" I asked.

He grabbed me around my neck, his hand so tight that I was choking. He let go. "Don't ask me any questions—do what I say," he said as he unzipped his pants. He made me give him a blow job, and I hated it. It felt like I couldn't breathe.

I stopped and pulled his pants back up when I heard a knock on the door. He opened the door to a Black man with a tall, stocky build, wearing a Chicago Bulls jersey and blue jeans. Michael introduced him to me as K-dog.

K-dog told me I looked sexy as hell, then walked back over to Michael and whispered in his ear. He said he wanted the whole job. My body went numb, knowing what that meant.

Michael said he would be back and kissed me on the forehead. I stood there staring, my eyes watery, but I held back the tears.

I was scared and wanted to get out. Then he pulled out his penis, and it was huge. I had never seen one that big, and immediately I grew extra nervous. Slowly, he pushed me onto the bed with a stained mattress.

In that moment, I felt like I couldn't do it. My mouth wasn't big enough, and I couldn't even think how to start. "Come on," he said in a persuasive voice. I knew if I didn't, Michael would be mad, so I tried, but I choked.

Without warning, he said he wanted anal sex. I told him I didn't want to, but he didn't care. He got on top of me and shoved it inside. He was rough, and I felt like my insides were falling out.

As the pain grew, I started praying for him to be done. I wanted to cry, but I held it in. I could feel my body going completely numb.

Michael came back into the room and told him to give it to me good. He just stood there watching. I looked at him with so much hate. I thought he loved me, but he was putting me through so much hurt. When I tried to get up because it hurt too much, K-dog said, "Where are you going, baby?"

He pulled me closer to his body. Then he stopped, pulled his penis out, and masturbated on the dirty bed. Finally, he was done. He got up and went to the bathroom while Michael still stood there watching.

I lay there with my black dress on; I never took it off. My body was in shock. Then K-dog came out and told Michael that that was some good young stuff. "See you next time," he said as he left.

I got up feeling sticky and sore. Michael threw $120 at me like I was some dog. "Good job, baby — you're making that money."

My mind raced. Why did I ever meet him? Why did I get myself into this, I wanted to kill myself and how am I going to get out? We left the hotel, and I couldn't speak; my voice was in shock. Why am I so stupid? Why do I let these men use me this way? First, I let my uncle use me. Now I let these men use me.

"You're getting really good at keeping me happy," Michael said.

That was his favorite thing to say; it became how I lived — always trying to please him to make him happy. I was young, and because of the abuse from my uncle, I didn't know any better. I felt I had to please men the same way I'd had to please my uncle.

I believed if I made them happy, they might not hurt me.

When I got home, Michael said he would call me tomorrow. My mom was asleep, so I went into the bathroom to shower — I wanted to wash it all off. I couldn't believe this was my life. There had to be something else, some other way to live; I just didn't know how to change things.

Standing in front of the mirror, I cried silently and held my hands to my face. Then I reached over to the tub and found a brown switchblade. I flicked it open, sat on the toilet, and held it to my wrist, but instead I cut my thigh. It started bleeding a little, and I stopped quickly. The pain felt like a strange relief.

I wanted to kill myself. I had thoughts of dying — maybe if I were gone, the pain would stop. I didn't want to live sometimes. After that, cutting happened now and then; it became a habit I didn't understand. I had never heard of anyone else doing it, but sometimes it eased the pain and quieted my thoughts.

Marketa Davis

I hid the scars just like the scars I carry on my heart. I knew they were there, but nobody else did. I never told anyone what I was doing.

That night I learned how to disappear — to smile in daylight while I bled in private. The next morning, I dressed and went back out, carrying that secret like a stone in my pocket.

CHAPTER 7

I remember when I started having intimate experiences at thirteen. It was all about being in control. It was a choice I made. Not the same as being forced, like when my Uncle James first assaulted me at ten. Back then, sex felt like a high; I would have it freely. I didn't care whom I slept with; I never enjoyed it.

But with Michael, I had no choice, no control anymore. It felt like I was being forced. I was just another object to Michael and all those men. I felt trapped and I couldn't get out. It was his game to play now — the game I didn't want to play anymore. I was so depressed, hurt, and confused again. How can someone say they love you and keep hurting you? Those were the same things Uncle James would tell me.

Sometimes I would sit in the corner of my room on the floor and just cry to myself. I would rock back and forth until cutting myself wasn't the answer anymore. It stopped easing my pain, and it felt like the pain stayed with me no matter what I did.

By spring of 1997, I was in the tenth grade, sitting in my History class, but the ache I'd carried never left me. My teacher's name was Ms. Hartford. She was Black and kind of tall, with her hair cut short and always curled. She dressed nicely and kept up with the latest fashions. She was kind of a cool teacher and sometimes let us keep our headphones to listen to music. Her classroom was decorated with Black art and African American images.

That day I was there but not really there — I wanted to be at home. I had been up all night talking to Michael on the phone; he wouldn't let me get off, and I finally fell asleep. Tina walked in late and sat down near me. She asked, "What's up? Where have you been? I haven't heard from you since we last talked." I told her I'd been around.

Then she snapped, "You think you're all that." Before I knew it she was yelling, "Since you're talking to Michael, you ain't nothing but a TRICK." The whole class started laughing. One girl, Lindsey, called me a "SLUT." I told her I wasn't a slut.

The word hit me like a punch. It reminded me of when my uncle raped me and used that same name. I had a flashback; I hated that word. I felt dirty and worthless. Tina kept going, asking, "Have you heard how you get around?"

Ms. Hartford heard the uproar and came back into the room. She asked what was going on, and by the time I stood up I was boiling hot — like a raging bull. I lost control.

I walked over and punched Lindsey in the face. She tried to hit me back, and we started fighting. In the chaos I grabbed Ms. Hartford's metal pencil sharpener from her desk and hurled it, but I missed. School security burst into the classroom to break us up. One guard grabbed me and pulled me back; I kicked and screamed for him to let me go as they pulled me into the hall.

I was trying to go back into the class where Lindsey was, but he took me to the office and into the room in the back. It was where they took kids when they got in trouble.

A few minutes later, the principal, Mrs. Peterson, came in. She was the meanest principal ever. She never liked me; she always said I was a troubled child. She asked, "What happened?" I told her the whole class was laughing, and then we started fighting. She said, "I'm going to call your mom. There's no fighting in my school. You are a troublemaker."

In my heart I wanted to shout, *But I'm not, Mrs. Peterson.* Everybody always thought I was a bad child. No one ever gave me a chance. It felt like people just hated me.

After some time, my mom finally got there. "Boy, oh boy," I heard her asking, "Where's my daughter?" You could hear the anger in her voice. The front desk clerk, Ms. Richards, brought her back to where I was.

The first thing she said was, "What happened? You're always getting in trouble. I'm sick of this." I told her Lindsey had called me a name, and I got mad. She said, "You shouldn't be fighting in school. I had to get off work, missing my money because of you."

My mom never listened to me. She never gave me a chance to explain what I had to say.

Soon after, the principal came back and started talking to my mom. She told her that I was suspended until further notice. The fight was bad. I had thrown that sharpener, and I could have hurt someone. She said that was like using a weapon.

I began to cry, begging Mrs. Peterson not to suspend me. "I'm sorry," she said. "I have to follow the school rules." My mom said, "Let's go."

As we walked toward the exit, I saw a classmate laughing at me. I just looked at her, and I wanted to punch her too. I was still so angry. I carried a lot of anger in me—once I got started, I didn't stop. But I was also hurt deep inside. I was going through so much, especially with Michael. I didn't know how to tell anyone what was going on. It was like keeping another secret, just as I did with my uncle. The more I tried to bury it, the more it came out in a burst of anger.

Later, when we got into the car, my mom said, "I still can't believe you were fighting in school. What were you thinking?" To be honest, I didn't know what to say. I was lost for words. I couldn't explain. It was hard to talk to my mom. I do know that when I get angry, I block it out. Sometimes I didn't even remember everything.

When we got home, I went straight to my room. I was walking fast up the stairs. My mom was still fussing, so I closed the door and turned my music on. I didn't really want to hear her anymore. My mom sometimes could go on and on like a broken record.

All I could think was, I can't wait until I'm grown and out of her house. I just stayed in my room the rest of the day. I didn't even come out—only to use the bathroom.

The next day, the school called. I was in my room asleep when my mom came in and opened the door quickly. She said, "Mrs. Peterson said they are trying to kick you out of all Detroit public schools." I jumped up and said, "No—that's not fair!" Why am I always getting treated so wrong? She said there was going to be a meeting at the school board at the end of the week. I got nervous, hoping they wouldn't kick me out.

Before she left, Mom said she was going to the casino — which had become her favorite place. I was glad she was going. She was still so mad at me that she just wouldn't let it go about school. She still blamed me and never took my side about what happened.

As soon as she left, I had to have a drink. I would hide brandy in a shoebox under my bed. I needed to relax and clear my mind. Soon after, Michael called and asked what I was doing. I said, "I'm just getting drunk while my mom is gone." Then he said he wanted to come over. I said that might not be a good idea — my mom could come back anytime. He said, "I need to see you. It's been a week; I miss you." He never took no for an answer, and I was scared of him.

In the end, I told him yes, he could come over. He said he would be there soon. I told him to park down the street because I didn't want anyone to see his truck in front of the house. He knocked on the door and came in. He grabbed me and started kissing me, telling me he missed me. We went to my room. He sat down on my bed and started talking. He said, "I got some weed I want you to sell for me." I said, "Weed? I can't do that — I'll get caught." He said, "You're not a baby. You're a woman. Be grown."

He always would still say that, but I was only seventeen.

"Remember, whatever I say goes. I'm your man. I'm in charge," he said.

Then he added, "I'll drop it off to you on Friday," trying to reassure me.

I was intimidated. I said, "Okay," in a really soft voice. It was like my words couldn't come out.

Then he asked, "What do you have for me?" I knew what that meant. Here we go again.

He told me to take off my clothes. I was taking them off very slowly. Then he started touching me and telling me how good I looked. I started to tremble.

Then he took off his pants but kept his shirt on. He told me to lay down on the bed. I lay down on my back, then he said, "The other way."

My throat tightened, and I was nervous and full of fear. He wanted anal — it was the first time he had asked for that. I told him I didn't want to do it, but he continued anyway.

Afterward, I kept thinking, "Please hurry," while holding back tears. Finally he said, "Baby, that was so good. I can't stay away that long. I always need you." I felt like garbage. I stayed lying there and told him he had to go because my mom might come home. He kissed me, smacked my butt, and said he'd see me on Friday.

I got up, sore, and ran a bath to try to wash the feeling away. It reminded me of what my uncle did. I sat in the tub a long time, staring at my wrinkled fingertips. When I got out and looked in the mirror, I told myself I was stupid and worthless for sleeping with Michael. I always let him, and afterward I felt dumb and hurt. He never loved me.

I didn't even know what love felt like, to be honest. I wished I had someone to talk to. I didn't have anyone—not even my sisters. Karla was kind of cool, but it was always hard to talk to Alison since she was grown and had a family of her own. We never had a real close relationship. When I was younger, I used to watch movies where sisters were close and loving. I longed for that kind of relationship with them. I would imagine that was me and my sisters. I used to pray and ask for us to be close together. I always wanted a close sister relationship, but I never got the love I yearned for.

Later that day, I heard my mom walk in. I was glad Michael was gone. Sneaking him into the house was dangerous. If she only knew, I would have been in big trouble. I was glad she never found out. People called my mom the mean mom. She was like a raging bull. In some ways, I was just like her whenever I got mad.

The next day came quickly—it was time for the school board meeting. I had to go to the school board on the West Side of Detroit. My mom was in her room getting ready.

I was still a bit sore, but I couldn't tell her, so I just dealt with it. I put on my favorite red jeans and white shirt.

My mom yelled upstairs that it was time to go. I came downstairs, and she was already in the car. When I got in, she said, "You better pray they don't kick you out." I just said, "I hope they don't either." She said, "I'm putting you back into counseling. Your anger is back." I didn't want to go see any dumb therapist. I hated them because they were nosy. All I ever did was sit, stare, and stay quiet.

We pulled up at the school board meeting. The building was big and tall. I got out of the car, feeling really nervous. We had to stop at the desk to see what floor the meeting was on. An older lady sat at the desk. She was white, with bright reddish lipstick, and wore an orange checkered blazer. She looked strange, almost like it was Halloween—even though it wasn't anywhere near the season.

We got on the elevator, and it seemed like we were riding forever. It was all the way up on the 16th floor.

We sat in the waiting area. They had a pretty water fountain shaped like an angel. A man came out to call us. He was a short Black man in a blue suit. The room was big, with long black tables. My mom and I sat down. The chairs were black. He introduced himself as Mr. White. He sat with a folder in his hand and began to read. I figured he was reading my file. He looked up and said, "I see you were fighting in school." I said yes. He asked me what happened, and I told him what had happened and what Lindsey called me. I could barely say the word — I hated thinking about it.

Then he warned me, "You know it was dangerous what you did — picking up a metal sharpener. Throwing it could have hurt someone." I said yes and that I was sorry. I was so angry and embarrassed by what I had done. I knew it was wrong. He said, "You know the board wants to kick you out of school. But I'm going to be lenient because I want you to stay in school. You have to promise you won't get into any more fights. I'm placing you on probation for six months. You better walk a thin line. And you have to keep your grades up, young lady."

My mom said, "I'm going to make sure she does that. I'm also putting her back into therapy." He looked at me and said, "Look at me and make that promise." I was nervous and my legs started shaking. I looked up and told him, "I promise I will not get in trouble again." The meeting was over, and he shook my hand with a tight grip. My mom said, "Thank you, Mr. White, for giving my daughter another chance."

We got back on the elevator and walked out to the car. The first thing my mom said was, "This is your last chance. You better not get in anything else. I think you need to be back on your medication." I thought to myself, I'm not getting back on medicine— I'm not going to be a zombie. I'll be eighteen soon. Medication wasn't the answer to my anger issues. What happened to me was the real issue. Also, part of my pain was about Michael being forced into doing things by a strong man who had so much power over me. I was an emotional wreck. I carried so much inside.

CHAPTER 8

It was a Friday in 1997. Michael called me to say he'd pick me up. When I answered the phone, he said, "Baby, I'll be there at 7 p.m." I paused for a moment, thinking to myself, I wish he would just disappear.

He said, "Do you hear me?"

I said, "Yes."

He said, "Next time act like it then."

All I heard was the dial tone when he hung up on me. I looked in my closet to see what I wanted to wear. It had to be something sexy — that's the way he always wanted me to dress. He said he wanted me to look older. I put on the tightest mini skirt I could find. I looked at the clock; it was almost 7 p.m. I hurried, wanting to be ready before my mom got home.

I walked out of the house and saw Ms. Hubert across the street. She was a Black woman with bright gray hair who watched everything on the block. I hated it when she saw me. I hoped she wouldn't tell my mom. She said, "Girl, where are you going with that skirt on? It's a little too short for you." I said, "I'm just going to hang out with my sister Karla." I knew if I said Karla, she wouldn't say anything to my mom.

From down the block I saw Michael pulling up. I started walking fast. I got to the corner and Mr. Jackson started talking to me. He creeped me out. He was Black with a huge Afro. He told me I looked nice in my skirt. I ignored him and kept walking. I thought he liked young girls — every time I saw him in a store he stared with those gloomy eyes and smiled in a way that made me uncomfortable.

I climbed into Michael's truck.

He said, "What was that man saying to you?" Michael hated seeing another man talk to me. I was like his possession. He would always say I was his and only his. I told him, "He just said he liked my skirt."

Why did I even say that?

Michael started saying, "You got these dirty men looking at you now, huh?" I said, "No, I don't. I didn't talk to him, I promise, I swear." My legs started shaking. I began to feel afraid, hoping he wouldn't hit me. When he got angry, that's what he always did.

Suddenly, his phone rang. I heard him say, "Okay, I might just have something for you." He pulled out two big bags of marijuana, handed them to me, and told me to put them in my purse.

We pulled up to a big yellow house. There were a bunch of cars outside. We got out of the car and walked up to the house. I remember one of the porch steps was missing, and I almost fell. I asked Michael whose house it was. He said it was his friend Red's.

A big chubby man answered the door, wearing a black shirt and blue jeans. Music was blasting inside. People were drinking and playing cards at the table. The whole house smelled like strong marijuana.

I sat down on a brown couch covered with cigarette burns. The walls were stained ivory white. A Black woman wearing leopard-print jeans walked over to me. She looked at me and asked who I was with. I told her, "Michael." She said I looked young. Then she handed me a joint and told me to hit it.

I looked at her and puffed it lightly. It was stronger than what I normally smoked. Something felt different, but I puffed it a couple more times. An instant high hit me.

Michael came over and asked for the two bags he had given me. Then he looked at me and said, "Baby, you high? You look messed up." He was drinking liquor and handed me a sip. Then he gave me a hundred-dollar bill, and I put it in my purse. He said, "That's for my baby!"

I sat there on the couch, trying to stay focused.

Later that night, a man came over and sat next to me. He was tall and kind of cute; he smelled really good and wore expensive glasses. I remember him saying his name was Eric — they called him E for short. He asked how old I was. I told him I was seventeen. He said, "What are you doing here?" I said, "I came with Michael — he's my boyfriend." Then he said, "I wish you were my girl. We could do so many things." He got up and walked away.

I kept drinking and smoking. When I got up to ask where the bathroom was, I was stumbling; the room was spinning. I saw Michael talking to Eric. They looked like two versions of the same person to me. I went over to Michael and asked where the bathroom was. He grabbed my hand and walked me upstairs. I stumbled a little on the stairs.

In the dark hallway, he showed me to the bathroom. I fumbled for the light switch while the room kept spinning. I nearly fell, but managed to steady myself. When I looked down, I saw needles on the floor. I don't know what they were. After I used the bathroom, I felt my way back toward the door. It was still dim, and Eric was standing outside. He said, "Michael said you had something for me." I was confused — Michael hadn't told me to give anything to anyone.

I kept walking, and Eric said, "Let me help you. You look like you need to lie down." He led me down a short hall to a bedroom. The room was dim, with a big bed and a bright red blanket. I felt dizzy and just fell onto the bed.

He said, "I was watching you when you came in. That skirt looks good on you." He grabbed my tights, rubbing them. I hit his hand. He slapped me and asked, "Are you gonna give it to me or what?"

I tried to get back up, but he pulled me down and hit me again. I cried, begging him to let me go. Each time I tried to get up, he pushed me back down. He climbed on top of me, and everything went blank. I didn't hear a sound. I couldn't hear anything.

When I came back to myself, my skirt and underwear were off. I was sore, and my legs ached. I didn't remember what happened. I scrambled to find my clothes on the other side of the room. Crying hysterically, I put them back on.

Downstairs, the house was almost empty. I looked for Michael, but he was gone. In the dining room I found a phone and called my friend Margo, sobbing and begging her to come get me. I told her I was scared. I had been drinking and getting high at one of Michael's friend's houses, but I couldn't even tell her the exact address. My mind couldn't think straight.

All I knew was there was a McDonald's on the corner and the cross streets were on the West Side of Detroit. I went outside and stood at the corner. It was still dark. Cars kept driving by, people asking if I needed a ride.

One old man pulled up in a black Cadillac. He was White, bald, wearing a Hawaiian shirt. He asked, "What are you doing out this time of night? It's 3 a.m.!" I thought, *3 a.m.—now my mom is really going to get me.* He asked if I needed a ride. I said, "No. I have a ride on the way."

He drove around in circles, making me nervous. I prayed, begging, *Please, Margo, hurry up.* Finally, she pulled up, and I jumped into her car as fast as I could. I was terrified. She looked at me and said, "What happened to you? You look like crap."

Honestly, I told her I didn't know. I couldn't remember. They gave me marijuana and drinks, but I had never felt like that before. I felt really weird. I just remembered a room and waking up. I told her

I couldn't go home. "Please take me to your house," I begged. She said her mom was out of town. That was a good thing. If her mom was home, she would tell my mom. The coast was clear, and I was glad about that. We got to her house.

The first thing I told her was that I wanted to take a shower. I felt so disgusting and nasty. She went into her room to get me something clean to put on. When she came out, she said, "Why did Michael leave you like that? You need to leave him alone. He has you all messed up. He doesn't care about you."

I said, "He loves me, and he gives me money." She said, "Yeah, he does, but he has you having sex with men for it. Look at you now. You can't even remember what happened to you."

Margo really made me think. I was so confused and hurt. I didn't know which way to go. I just wanted to live a happy teenage life. Instead, I was forced to be a grown woman when I wasn't. I was always forced to be something I wasn't.

I went into the bathroom to get in the shower. I looked up and saw a bruise around my neck. I couldn't remember how it got there, but I knew I had to hide it. I ran the shower hot and started to scrub my body, crying, trying to wash the nasty feeling away and asking God to help me get out of this relationship with Michael.

I heard a knock at the door. It was Margo asking me if I was okay. I said, "Yes, I'll be out in a minute." I kept scrubbing.

When I got out of the shower, I put on the clothes Margo gave me. It was her favorite pair of gym shorts. She played basketball. I went into her room, and she told me I could sleep in her bed while she slept on the floor.

I lay in her bed, so exhausted. What a long night. All I remember was her saying, "Good night, get some rest. I love you." I fell asleep fast.

I woke up that morning feeling so sick I ran to the bathroom and kept throwing up. Margo gave me some orange juice in the bathroom. I told her I had to get home. I wanted to get there before my mom woke up; she usually slept late. Margo got dressed, and I went outside to sit on the porch.

We got in Margo's silver Honda Civic, but it didn't want to start. She tried again; on the third crank it finally turned over. Thank God. When we pulled up to my house, Johnny's car was there, which felt like a relief. I got out of the car; Margo said, "Call me later."

I stepped onto the front porch and heard my mom's dog barking. She had a teacup, apricot-colored poodle named Pierre; he always got on my nerves. When I opened the front door slowly, he stopped barking when he saw it was me and ran up the stairs. I closed the door and crept up to my room at the end of the hall, passing my mom's closed door. I changed quickly, put on my nightgown, and went back to sleep.

The phone rang, and Michael called, apologizing for why he left me. He said he had to go back on a drug run. I didn't care; I just listened while dozing. He yelled on the phone, "Don't you hear me?" I answered softly, "Yes." He said he wanted to come get me later and that he had a job for me to do. I told him no — I couldn't do it. My mom had something for me to do later; I made up a random lie.

I was tired and hurting. I was tired of men using my body. I didn't care about the money. I still couldn't remember what happened last night. I told him maybe next time. He got angry and hung up, saying, "Remember, I own you." That scared me.

A flashback hit me — it brought back when he first hit me in his truck. My mom woke up and came into my room. She told me I had to clean up the kitchen. You know it was Saturday, and that was clean-up day. I lay there, not wanting to move. But I couldn't tell her that — if I did, I probably would get a slap across my face. She said we were having a BBQ and my aunts were coming over later. I still wasn't feeling anything at all. I wanted to stay in my bedroom all day. Now the whole family was coming over — oh gosh.

There wasn't going to be any resting for me. Everything had to be perfect — just the way my mom liked it. I went into the kitchen to start cleaning and wash the dishes. Then Johnny came in. He said, "Good afternoon," and I said hi. He fixed himself some coffee and started asking what I'd been up to. I said nothing — just school and trying to stay out of trouble. Sometimes you had to keep it simple with Johnny; he could run his mouth nonstop. I hurried to finish cleaning. I wanted to go back upstairs.

My mom came downstairs and gave Johnny a list of things to get from the store. She went outside to water the grass. I finished cleaning the kitchen. The phone rang; I walked right past it. My mom yelled for me to answer. I picked it up; it was my Aunt Paula. She asked where my mom was, and I told her she was outside. I handed the phone to my mom. Aunt Paula asked who was on the phone, and I said it was her. Then I went back upstairs to my room and got back in bed.

I watched TV for a little while. When the movie *House Party* came on, I dozed off. I slept for a good while. My door burst open — it was my sister Alison. I couldn't win that day. She started, "Girl, why are you still in bed?" I told her to mind her business and to leave me alone. I threw my pillow at her and then tried to go back to sleep.

When I finally woke up, I got up to take a shower. I heard voices downstairs — a man's voice; it wasn't Johnny's. I looked at the clock: it was 3 p.m. I had almost slept the day away. I stayed in the shower a long time. When I got out, I still saw that bruise on my neck. It wasn't very noticeable, but I could tell it was there — and I hated it. I got dressed in my orange sundress — my lounge dress for the day. I didn't care what I put on.

I went downstairs. My mom was in the kitchen cutting up greens, and my Aunt Paula was helping. She said hello and hugged me.

My Aunt Paula was so pretty. She had the prettiest skin. Her skin complexion was caramel. My mom told me to help snap the green beans. I just wanted to sit down on the couch. I started snapping the green beans and putting them in the bowl. I heard Johnny and some guys outside laughing. I got up to look outside and saw Uncle James. I dropped the bowl from my hand. My mom started yelling, "What's wrong with you, girl?" It was like I saw a ghost.

I thought, "What is he doing here?" It felt like I was still being tortured by this big monster who had taken everything from me as a child. The old fear washed over me. I was still so scared of him. My mom told me to clean up the mess. I picked the beans up as fast as I could.

Uncle James and Johnny came in with beers in their hands. Uncle James spoke to me in his stern voice, but I ignored him. He expected girls to come hug their uncle. He grabbed me and hugged me tight. I pulled away. He tried to talk to me. That's what he always did when I saw him; it seemed to give him pleasure. I looked at my mom and she was talking to Johnny. My Aunt Paula went outside. I wanted my mom to notice — to see the fear I felt when he came around, like a mother should.

All these years she still hadn't noticed. He walked away and said, "You will always be my favorite niece, no matter how grown you get." I went to the phone and called Margo to come get me. She said she'd be there in a minute. I wasn't going to stay anywhere near the man who abused me. My life was already messed up because of him. I hated family gatherings.

I left that house determined to get away — I would not let him ruin me again.

CHAPTER 9

I felt like I was going to lose my mind after seeing my Uncle James. It was hard for me to think. I became scared all over again — traumatized. I started feeling just like I did when I was a little girl. How could the man who hurt me so badly still be allowed to walk this earth? I wished I had a voice back then, that I had told someone.

Instead, I immediately blamed myself again. I called myself stupid and tore myself down. That's how bad I felt, thinking it was still my fault.

Just then, Margo pulled up to get me. My mom was in the backyard, and I didn't dare go back there where she was — Uncle James was still there. I told myself, forget it. I'll call my mom later and tell her I'm staying over at Margo's house.

My mind was all over the place. I realized I had forgotten to pack clothes. I ran upstairs quickly and grabbed enough for a couple of days. When I came back down, I heard my mom in the kitchen. I went into the dining room and told her Margo was there and I was going to her house.

Instantly, she got mad. "The family is over and you're just going to leave? I cooked all this food," she said. I wanted to tell her, *Well, your brother James is here — the one who abused me. You never paid attention enough to notice anything.* I wanted to tell her so badly, but the words wouldn't come out.

Instead, I told her Margo and her cousins were going to the video arcade and I'd be back later. But little did she know, I was leaving for a few days.

When I got in the car, Margo asked what took me so long. I told her I had to pack my bags. She noticed I was breathing hard and said, "What's up with you? You act like you're scared for your life! Who scared you?"

I paused. "Oh, nothing," I said. "I was just trying to get out of that house." I started crying. Margo asked what was wrong again, but I told her nothing. She said, "We've been friends since elementary school. What are you so afraid of? I know you."

I listened, thinking to myself, *Should I tell her about Uncle James?* The words were there, but I couldn't get them out. Finally, I told her that if I shared a secret, she had to promise not to tell anyone. I was still living in shame — embarrassed, not wanting anyone to know.

I told her it was about my Uncle James.

"What about him?" she asked.

"When I was little, he used to touch me." Suddenly, she slammed on the brakes and pulled over.

"WHAT?" she screamed, staring at me in shock.

I repeated, "He used to touch me. He used to rape me almost every day. It started when I was seven—when he was babysitting me. My mom would be at work. It happened every chance he got. I was so scared to tell anyone. He always told me not to tell."

I looked over at Margo and she was crying. She said she was so sorry for what happened to me. I told her that's why I didn't want to stay at home. That is why I called her to come get me. I hated being there when he was there.

She asked, "He used to do all that to you?" "Yes."

"The actual thing?" I said, "Yes."

"Your mama didn't know anything?" "No."

"What about your sisters?" "No."

I told her I was all alone. I had no one to help me. I hated what he did to me. I hated it. It felt like a little relief. I told Margo, but somehow the pain was still there. She was my friend — like a sister to me. She said, "You need to tell your mom."

"I can't — I'm scared to tell her," I said. "What if she doesn't believe me? My mom loved her brother and would do anything for him. My mom was the type of person you couldn't go to. She was so mean. I was afraid."

Big tears rolled down Margo's face. She said, "I still think you should tell her." "I don't want to talk about it anymore," I replied. "I need a drink."

"We can go over to my boyfriend's house," she offered.

Her boyfriend's name was Martin. He was tall, dark-skinned, and kind of cute. I said, "Okay." We started driving and stopped at the gas station near Warren Ave on the Westside of Detroit — the neighborhood where we'd grown up. Margo got out to pay for the gas. Shortly after, I heard loud music. I looked out the window and saw Michael pull up. I slid down in the seat; I didn't want him to see me.

I hadn't spoken with him since the last time we were on the phone, when he left me at his friend's house. I got scared and thought, "Please hurry up, Margo." I looked up and saw him standing, talking to a man. He was yelling at him, really loud, telling him to pay what he owed. Michael was furious.

Margo came back out. I looked up and said, "Look — Michael is over there." She hurried, still pumping gas. I heard Michael's voice draw closer; he said, "Margo, is that you?"

"Yes," she answered, still pumping the gas.

Michael's voice grew sharper. "Have you talked to her?"

She said, "Yes — last week I did." I was in the car, shivering.

He walked closer to the car and asked her to call me. "She hasn't been answering the phone for me." Then, all of a sudden, he looked in the car and I was almost on the floor. He started yelling, "This is how you play me? Ducking and dodging me — not calling me? Not answering the phone." He yells, "Get out of the car right now!"

I'm crying, saying, "No, I can't get out."

He said, "Don't make me get you out of that car."

Margo started saying, "Leave her alone. Just leave her alone. That was cold how you left her at that house."

He told her, "Little girl, mind your business. This is my girl."

He opened the door quickly and I slightly fell out. He grabbed me by my arm. Margo yelled, "Leave her alone and let her go!"

I could see people looking, but no one helped.

"Please let me go. You're hurting my arm," I cried.

He opened his truck door and told me to get in. My legs were stiff; I couldn't move them. I heard Margo continue to say, "Leave her alone!"

I could finally lift one foot up into his truck. His girl got in now. I got in and he said, "I don't know why you are trying to play me. Let me make this clear: I own you. You are mine."

He drove off fast. I was still crying; I was so scared. Please help me...anybody...

Michael said, "You've been ignoring me, huh?" "No, I was just on punishment."

I just made up something to say — I couldn't tell him the truth. I didn't want to make him more upset. We pulled up at his house. He yelled at me to get out. I got out of the car slowly. We went into the house and I sat down at the table. He told me, "I thought you loved me."

I said, "I do."

How could I love a man who hurt me? I was used to being hurt. He started telling me, as always, how he missed me and how he apologized for leaving me at his friend's house. That was his way of trying to be nice. It was another form of manipulation — something he was so good at. Then he led us both upstairs to his room.

The first thing he said was, "I have a job for you to do. My friends will be over later." I wasn't up for any job. I pleaded with him not to give me any more jobs. He pushed me to the floor so fast that it felt like the wind got knocked out of me. Then he started kicking me in my side. I was yelling and crying for him to stop — please, stop. "How many times do I have to tell you to do what I say?" he yelled in my face.

After that, his abuse seemed to get worse. He told me to get up, but I couldn't; my ribs hurt too much — it hurt to breathe. I tried to tell him I couldn't take this anymore, but he just said I could and would take whatever. I crawled to the bed, stood, and then fell onto it. He went into a drawer, threw some lingerie at me, and told me to put it on. I remember it being pink with lace. He then left the room.

I sat for a moment, trying to figure out how to escape. I looked around for his cell phone — maybe I could call Margo or my sister, Karla. I hurried to put the lingerie on before he came back because I didn't want to make him any angrier, though I could still barely move. After dressing, I lay on his bed, curled in a ball, trying to ease the pain.

I lay there for what seemed like hours. Then the door opened and Michael returned, smelling of marijuana and carrying a glass of brandy. He sat down beside me and told me to sip the drink and take a hit from the joint. I did what he told me. I puffed it twice and began choking, and then he gave me another sip of liquor.

That outer-space feeling returned like before. I just lay back down. I looked up at the ceiling; the room was spinning — it seemed to sway back and forth. He told me to relax and clear my mind. His door opened and a man came in, but I couldn't lift my head to see him clearly. A Black man, very tall and slim, wearing a blue suit. I heard Michael say, "Just take your time. She's sweet and young and never says his name." Then he left the room.

The man came over to the bed and began unbuttoning his shirt, then took off his pants until he was down to nothing. All I remember is him shoving his penis in my mouth. I gasped for air and tried to sit up, but he pushed me back down. Then he got on top of me and said, "Let's get this job done right. This is what I'm paying for." He started having sex with me. I lay there, not making a sound. He moaned and sweated, pulling me close; I tried to pull away but he yanked me back. "Are you trying to run from me? We can do this all night, baby," he taunted. My body felt crushed under his weight.

He stopped, reached into his coat pocket, and brought out a small white bag of powder. He set it on Michael's dresser, knelt, took a clear straw, and sniffed. He told me he was ready for more. I cried that I wanted to stop, but he said, "The party's just getting started." He turned Michael's radio up loudly and forced me back down on the bed. He was rough as he climbed on top of me again, grabbing my wrist tight and kissing me, trying to force his tongue into my mouth. He pushed and pushed. I kept telling him to wait, but he wouldn't stop. It felt like hell.

I stared at the window and saw how dark it was outside. I had to get out of there, but he kept going.

I was trying to get up again when he grabbed me by the neck and pushed me back down. As he finished up, he said, "I gotta tell Michael I liked you. I need you the next time."

He started putting on his clothes, then reached into his pocket and gave me $120.

That was always for the whole job — my worth — but it wasn't worth any of it.

Michael came back into the room. He got in the bed behind me and put his arm around me. What a disgusting feeling I had. I got up and told him that I needed to take a shower. He made me wait a minute before giving me an old shirt to put on. I had no clothes because I left my bag in Margo's car.

I went into his bathroom and saw the same powdery bag the man had used. I knew it was some type of drug.

That outer-space feeling hung on. I turned on the shower; my body was so sore all over. I got in and just sat down, rocking back and forth. I looked over and saw Michael's razor. I thought about cutting myself so badly; I needed to ease my pain. I promised I wouldn't hurt myself again, but it was very tempting. I was so lost, imagining all the pain I'd gone through as a little girl. Now, as a teen, I was still going through hell. No one ever cared about me — that's what I always believed.

I turned off the shower, opened the curtain, and stepped out. Michael was standing right at the door, just staring at me. He scared me terribly; I could hardly breathe. It was creepy how he looked at me as I got dressed. He led me back over to the bed and I said to him, "Michael, I'm so tired. I just want to go to bed, please."

He said, "Ok, tomorrow we can. But what about just 10 minutes of oral sex baby." He grabs my head and makes me go down. I was tired and disgusted by it all; I hated it. After it was over, I ran to the bathroom so fast. I started washing my mouth out and gagging. I think I brushed my teeth five times.

I went back into the room where he had fallen asleep. I lay there, thinking about when I was going to get away from him. He made me feel awful; he kept hitting me and I felt hopeless. I cried myself to sleep that night.

The next morning I woke to find him getting ready for work in the bathroom. I called Margo—no answer; I called again with the same result. I wanted to go to her house; I knew she was worried about me. I didn't want to go home, but I had no choice, I had nowhere else to go. I started getting dressed, and he came back into the room, ready to leave. He asked where I was going, but I told him to take me home. I kept wishing Margo would have answered the phone.

When we got to the corner of my street, he reached over and kissed me, telling me he loved me and that he'd call me later. I looked back; I couldn't even say it back to him. I just got out of the car and started walking home, praying my mom wouldn't be there.

I kept walking until I passed Mario's house. He was a neighborhood boy who lived down the street. He played on the high school football team and thought he was so fine just because he had muscles. I walked past his house while he was washing a truck. He said "What's up?" and I said hello back and kept walking. He asked when I wanted to hang out, and I told him I didn't know, but soon. I think he had a little crush on me because he always seemed to flirt when I saw him.

When I got to my porch, I didn't hear any barking, which meant my mom had Pierre with her — yes! She wasn't home. I heard Ms. Hubert say, "Your mama's not home. She went around to your grandma's house." She is so nosy. She just sat on that porch in that old black rocking chair like the neighborhood watch.

The first thing I did was go into the kitchen to get something to eat. It felt like I hadn't eaten in days. I heated up the leftover chicken and some greens my mom had cooked. I was so hungry, though I hadn't had much of an appetite yesterday after everything that happened. After I finished, I cleaned up the kitchen; I wanted to make sure I wouldn't hear my mom's mouth — you know how that is!

A sharp pain stabbed my side where Michael had kicked me. I went into the bathroom to get something for the pain. It happened suddenly, the pain coming out of nowhere.

I didn't want to tell my mom because I was still too scared. I went up the stairs to my room and tried calling Margo again, but her mom answered and said she wasn't there. I asked her mom to please have Margo call me back. I tried to relax by watching TV and writing in my journal — I thought that might help; writing had helped me before when I was a kid. I needed help so badly. I needed to be rescued from Michael.

The pen drops out of my hand as I drift to sleep; I was so sleepy. The door shuts at the bottom of the stairs and I am immediately awake. I was a light sleeper, having trained myself, when I was a little girl, to always be aware because of the persistent fear I felt in the house. I told myself, "Oh, it's probably my mom coming back from my grandma's house or maybe one of my sisters — who knows?"

I heard a noise in the kitchen, and then it went quiet. I just kept on lying in my bed. I heard footsteps coming up the stairs; the steps were squeaking. We had wooden floors, so you could hear really well when someone was coming up the stairs. Then I heard a man's voice — it sounded like he was talking on the phone. I knew it wasn't Johnny because my mom's boyfriend never came over when she wasn't there.

I got up and cracked my door a little to look out. I didn't see anyone, but I heard footsteps in the hallway right in front of the bathroom. The bathroom was right by my bedroom door, so I looked out again. It was my Uncle James. My heart almost dropped. Oh my God — what is he doing here?

After I saw him, I eased the door closed, but not quietly enough — he heard it. He called, "Who's here?" I didn't say anything; I was shaking in the corner of my room. He opened the door, and my eyes grew large. My bladder stopped working. He said, "What are you doing here? Your mom said you were gone over your friends." I stood there frozen, unable to move, unable to talk — my voice gone.

"You hear me talking to you?"

I couldn't really speak; it felt like I was a little girl again. That fear was still there; I was so scared of him. I could feel the pee running down my legs.

"I'm glad you're back home. Your mama was upset. You can't be making her upset. She was so mad you left that day. Don't you miss your family? I missed you. You turned out to be even nicer. You're still my favorite niece. Don't act like you are all grown now."

Then he said, "I'm gonna be here for a little while. I lost my place. Your mom said I could sleep in the basement."

He walked out of my room, and I locked my door quickly. Why did he have to move back in? Just why? What do I do now? I didn't come back out of my room until my mom came back home. I sat there feeling scared and alone. I prayed he wouldn't come into my room and hurt me. Why me again?

Morning came slowly, and with it a weight of decisions I didn't yet know how to carry.

CHAPTER 10

I often wished that somebody could have protected me from my uncle. I used to imagine someone catching him in the act. I was so sad and so alone. I cried for help inside my head. It wasn't fair that I had to endure all of it. I was just a child. I lived through my abuse alone and went through so much pain and heartache. Most of all, I carried so much shame. I felt embarrassed about what happened to me; I wanted to explode inside. He walked around so freely, as if he had done nothing wrong. People had no idea of what a true monster he really was.

One time I came home and saw Uncle James sitting on the couch, drinking his beer. He looked at me, then spoke to me and winked. He even smiled; it turned my stomach and made me so sick. I ran upstairs to the bathroom and started throwing up. That's how sick he made me feel just by the sight of him. My heart would pound so hard—like my chest was about to fall out. The fear of him was unbearable. It was something that no one would ever want to feel. No matter how hard I tried to push it out of my mind, it resurfaced time after time. The memories were so disgusting, and I became traumatized all over again. I couldn't eat, and I cried a lot when I was alone. I didn't want anyone to see me.

At night I started doing it again—keeping my door locked. I would put my desk behind my door to make sure he couldn't get in. Sometimes I would just sit and watch my door. The nightmares came back, waking me in sweats, crying and rocking just like I would when I was a little girl. I learned to go into survival mode. As a child, I had taught myself a lot, having to handle so much without a choice. I was all by myself, facing adult things. More than anything, all I ever wanted was to be saved.

I remember being so upset when I asked my mom about Uncle James moving back in. I asked her why he was there and told her I didn't like him, that he drank too much and she always catered to him. But nothing changed.

She only said to me that he was her brother and needed a place to live. I yelled so loud that I told her I hated him being here. She never even asked why. She just got mad and said that this was her house and that she could have anyone in her house if she wanted to. She went on and on. I was so mad; I was distraught and stormed away. It was never an ending story with my mom. Once she made up her mind about something, that's what went.

I wanted her to stop me so badly. I wanted her to just hug me and say, "Baby, what's wrong? It's gonna be okay. I love you." Maybe then I would have broken my silence and told her what had happened. I wanted love, and I couldn't get it from her. I didn't feel loved at all; I felt unworthy. I just wanted to disappear.

Right after he moved in, Uncle James started harassing me. He would say little things like, "You look good in those jeans," and, "You filled in nicely since you were a little girl." I tried my best to ignore him. My voice felt permanently stuck, and I could never get it back — my body in perpetual shock.

One day, while my mom was at work, Uncle James came home drunk. I was in the kitchen washing dishes, and he was stumbling toward me. I started shaking, nervous and scared. I hurried to finish the dishes.

He came up behind me and asked where my mom was. I told him she was at work in a little, soft voice. I was still trembling. He said, "Don't be afraid," and started rubbing my shoulders. I was drying a glass and remember dropping it on the floor. The glass shattered, so I bent down to pick it up. He grabbed my arm and pulled me back up. I pulled my arm away and started walking off. I was in the dining room when he shoved me into the corner. I started telling him to please leave me alone.

He grabbed my breast and squeezed. He told me that I had developed so nicely, that I was so beautiful and still so special to him. I pulled away, and he forced me back against the wall. I cried, telling him to let me go. He said, "Or what?" and I froze — I couldn't move. He started unzipping his pants while holding me there. I screamed, and he told me to be quiet.

Suddenly, a little strength came back and I pulled away, falling to the floor. He yanked my legs toward him. I was still yelling and fighting to escape, but he was so strong.

He kept saying that I was gonna give it to him, and I knew what that meant. He always said that to me right before he would assault me. Those words are always stuck in my head. I used my knee to strike him in his stomach. He called me a stupid little slut and told me I would always be dirty. I got up and ran up the stairs to my bedroom.

I locked my door. I pushed the dresser and whatever else I could find in front of the door and cried in the corner. I was shaking and rocking. I don't know what happened, but he didn't try to come after me. I sat there asking God to please help me; I was so scared. That was the day Uncle James attempted to rape me again.

I couldn't let that ever happen to me again. I couldn't let him hurt me anymore. I became so paranoid — it felt like I was reliving the trauma all over again. I felt like a helpless little girl. It was like I was playing by his rules. I thought it was over when he moved out. I thought I would never have to live that way again. He was gone.

When he moved out I was eleven. I was bigger now. I was stronger now. Still, I felt powerless and voiceless. In my mind it was like he was raping me all over again. I don't know what happened, but he didn't bother me the rest of the day. I prayed that I had scared him away. I hoped he didn't touch me again. I had so much hate for him. He was a monster who deserved to be punished. I wanted him to go to jail so bad. I wanted him to go away and never come back. He ruined my life.

I still couldn't tell another soul. I hated myself for that. I blamed myself so much. My silence only made it feel like I was being abused again. I thought back to when I told Margo and when I told my teacher in middle school. Why was I still so scared to tell my mom or anybody else? I asked myself, "Why was it shameful?" I realized it was all I knew.

It was wrong and a crime, and I'm old enough to know that now. There was so much shame and guilt. Why did I feel guilty? It was something he did to me. I beat myself up as a child for not telling anyone about my abuse. I gave my mom plenty of signs. I begged her to stay whenever she would leave me alone with him, and I even started wetting the bed. I tried so hard for her to notice something — anything. My mom didn't want to ask or say anything. I believe she was in her own world.

Sometimes, I ask myself, "Did she even know?"

That puzzled me so much. I started cutting myself again. I remember sitting on the bathroom floor one night, sobbing as crazy thoughts raced through my head. I told myself I didn't want to cut, but I found myself doing it again. I needed to ease my pain. It was either cutting myself or drinking, and I chose to cut.

In that moment, I really wanted to die. I figured, what in my life did I have to live for? I took the razor and placed it against the upper part of my wrist. I pressed hard against my skin until I saw a little blood. I continued to cry, asking God to help me again. I didn't want to live anymore, but something just stopped me. I couldn't go through with it. I jumped up, turned the bathroom sink on, and rinsed the blood from my arm. I wrapped a towel around my wrist to stop the bleeding. It was terrifying. The bleeding slowed, and I sat back on the bathroom floor a little longer, just crying to myself, saying, "Please — I just want all this to go away."

I didn't want to hurt anymore. I expressed my anger in wanting to commit suicide so badly again. Inflicting pain on myself was my way of treating the hurt. I believed the lies and told myself it would cure me. It never solved anything.

I got up and went into my room and locked myself in. I stayed up all night worrying — afraid Uncle James might come into my room. I was so afraid to close my eyes; the memories from my abuse kept replaying in my head. It was triggering. I wanted to disconnect my mind from my body; I wished I were invisible. I couldn't keep my eyes open any longer. When I finally fell asleep, it was daylight. I could hear the birds chirping at my window. They sounded so sweet and pleasant — if only my life were pleasant and not feeling like hell.

I used to think I was unlovable. I thought I was born not to be loved; I believed I was a piece of trash. I would tell myself, "You're a bad person." I wasn't aware of how cruel my attitude was toward myself. I always felt completely useless. I was a girl who didn't know how to express her emotions; I had been taught to keep quiet. My anxiety and depression grew. I didn't want to do anything but go to school and stay in my room. I even turned to liquor again. Part of drinking still made me feel at ease. I wanted to erase the pain I was feeling.

The dirty flashbacks of Uncle James never stopped. The visions haunted me and wouldn't go away. My mind was paralyzed, trapped in fear, guilt, and shame. One night, Margo called, and I was so glad to hear from her. I hadn't spoken to her in a few months, and she told me she was coming over to see me. I missed her so much. I really needed her. I had been going through a lot since Uncle James had moved back in, and I longed for comfort. Most of all, I needed someone who would listen to me. She was the only one who knew my secret.

When she came over, I opened the door and instantly fell into her arms, crying. She asked what was wrong. I told her Uncle James had moved back in and how he had been harassing me—how he tried to take advantage of me again. I told her to go upstairs in case he came home. She said, "Girl, what are you gonna do? You have to get out of here."

I didn't know what to do or where I would go. I didn't want to call Michael. I didn't want to go with him. He was abusing me too and making me sell my body. I wanted to stay clear of him. I was glad I hadn't talked to him.

We both cried together and then talked. I even laughed, remembering the good days. We used to do some crazy stuff when we were kids.

Suddenly, it was time for her to go. I hated that she had to leave, but she needed to pick her mom up from work. I walked her down the stairs, and we gave each other a big hug. She said we were going to come up with a plan. I didn't know what the plan was, but I needed it fast.

She told me she would call me later. I was hurt that she had to go. It seemed like my happiness just disappeared, and I was sad again. I went back up the stairs. I wanted to take a bath and just go to bed. I got my night clothes and went into the bathroom to run my water. I started to pray, talking to myself, and asking God why I was such a bad person. I repeatedly asked Him why I deserved the things that happened. I think I stayed in the bath for hours. I remember my fingertips were wrinkled. It was about time for me to get out.

When I got out, I looked in the mirror. I asked myself, "Why were you such a stupid little girl? Why did you let Uncle James hurt you? You must be crazy, just like people thought you were."

Teardrops rolled down my face.

I opened the door and saw Uncle James in my mom's room. Her room was right across from the bathroom. My heart fell to the floor. He turned around and looked at me as if I had scared him. He was going through my mom's drawings for some reason. Then he started walking toward me, so I hurried to my room, trying to lock the door. He yelled, "Don't you walk away from me! I haven't forgotten what you did to me the other day. I see you got smart now?"

I told him to please leave me alone. He reached and grabbed my shirt while grabbing my butt. He pulled me closer and kissed me on the back of my neck. He covered my mouth while I yelled at him to let me go. He tried to push me onto my bed, and I grabbed the doorway to keep myself from being pulled into my room. I tried to fight him off, but he wouldn't let me go.

He pushed me down in the hallway, and my head hit the floor. I thought I was about to black out. He got on top of me, trying to pull my pants down. I started kicking even harder. You could smell the alcohol on him. I heard the downstairs door open, and he covered my mouth. It was my mom who called my name. He whispered, "You better not say anything." He got up, looked, put his finger to his lips, walked away, and went downstairs to talk to my mom.

I got up and went into the bathroom to wash my face. I didn't want my mom to see me crying. I was scared that he would kill me or hurt me again. I was afraid because he was so powerful. I had to keep quiet. My mom came up the stairs as I left the bathroom. She told me that she was calling for me. I lied and told her that I didn't hear her, that I had my door closed and the music was on. I had to protect myself. I didn't know what else would happen.

Sometimes I wanted it all to be a dream so I could wake up and it would all be over. But this was my reality; it wasn't a dream. My life still went on while I lived in fear. If only you could imagine how I felt — it was horrible. I was terrorized and tortured by this man, first in my childhood and now as a teenager. I was angry and had so much hate building up inside that I wanted to explode. That feeling was frightening sometimes.

The little girl I was carrying inside wanted to be released; she couldn't bear the burden any longer. Self-harming made me feel so numb inside. The more I did it, the more it gave me something like a high. For some reason, it reminded me I was alive. I wanted to punish my body. I felt disgusted with myself. When my Uncle James assaulted me as a little girl, I dealt a way to disassociate from my body. That's how I dealt with the pain. The feelings of shame were still there, but my mind wasn't.

As I got older, self-harming, drinking, and smoking were new ways for me to cope and drown out the pain. It was the only way out that helped me keep everything inside. I didn't know how to escape. It felt like the end for me. My life was a never-ending story. I felt like I didn't deserve to breathe; I didn't deserve life. What was the point of being on this earth? There wasn't a day that went by that I didn't want to die. My depression continued to worsen.

I had experienced so much that I shouldn't have. People didn't understand what I was going through. I felt like a doormat; people just walked over me and never noticed anything. There were constant screams in my head, crying out for help, but nothing ever came out. Sometimes I wish I had been taught how to express myself when I was a little girl. I wish I had been taught self-love; no one ever talked about anything. Maybe if I had been taught about good and bad touches at home, I would have told an adult what my Uncle James was doing to me.

I didn't have a clue about what was going on, but I knew in my heart that it was wrong because of the pain I would be in afterward. Maybe that's why I kept it all inside—because my mom didn't teach me. The only way I learned about sexual abuse was later in school. Finally, I discovered that what Uncle James was doing was wrong.

Now what was I going to do about it since he's moved back in? Who would believe me? He had made two attempts to rape me. The evil monster had to be stopped. Where was my voice? Would I ever get the strength to speak?

I didn't know the answer then — only that I had to try.

CHAPTER 11

Every day it seemed like I was fighting for my life. I was fighting to be saved from my Uncle James. I was so tired of him. I didn't know what to do anymore. My anger had built up in an awful way. I was full of rage and didn't know how to control it. I started taking my anger out on anyone. It became the only way I knew how to get attention.

As time went on, life outside of home carried its own battles. I remember that in 1998, I was roller skating with Margo. The skating rink was on the East Side of Detroit. There was this girl named Lauren, who was very fashionable, always wearing the latest brands, and people called her a spoiled brat. Her mom and dad bought her anything she wanted. She used to hang out with my old friend Tina in school. We never used to get along because she always thought she was better than other people. She used to get smart with me and call me names. One time she called me a trick, and I got so angry, but I knew I couldn't get in trouble in school again.

That day at the skating rink, tensions rose quickly. When Margo and I walked up to the skating rink, I looked over and saw her sitting on the bench. I could see her whispering in another girl's ear, and they both looked at me and laughed. I walked past them, and they just stared. I wanted to say something so bad. While I was walking, Lauren's friend got up and walked past me, lightly bumping into me. I told her that she better watch it.

She said, "Watch what?" I said, "You heard me."

At that moment, anger took over. I could feel my insides boiling; I was getting so mad. I went to the counter to get my skates. I turned around, looking for Margo, and saw her talking to her boyfriend. I started skating down the aisle, and Lauren stuck her feet out. I hit the floor so hard, and all I heard was everyone laughing at me. I got up and pushed her to the floor. I lashed out at her and slapped her. I was just that angry. I could hear everyone around us saying, "Fight! Fight!"

Before long, an intervention came. This older lady came out of nowhere and pulled me off her. I remember her telling me, "You are such an angry young lady. You are too beautiful to be this angry." She seemed so nurturing, and her voice was so soft.

I said, "I don't care. She tripped me. She shouldn't have done that to me."

I quickly snatched away from the lady and told her she wasn't my mama. Margo and her boyfriend came running over to where I was, and I saw security following.

The night escalated even more. They told Lauren and me that we had to leave, and they would call our parents if we didn't leave. It didn't matter at that time; I was ready to fight Lauren and her friend. I didn't care about anything at that moment—that's how steamed I was inside. We left the roller rink.

Afterward, the weight of my choices hit me. Margo was kind of mad at me for getting into the fight. She told me that I had spoiled it for us. I felt so bad because I knew how much she loved to skate. Margo dropped me off at home, and I angrily walked in and slammed the door. Before I knew it, my mom was yelling at the top of her lungs. She said, "Girl, you better stop slamming my door!"

My mom was cooking dinner before work in the kitchen, and it smelled delicious. I wanted her to stay home, but she had to pay the bills. I told her I was mad, and she asked why. I told her I had gotten into a little fight at the skating rink because this girl from school tripped me on purpose and embarrassed me in front of everybody there. She instantly blamed me and said, "You shouldn't be fighting. You walk around here always so damn angry."

But the anger wasn't really about the skating rink. I was angry because of Uncle James. She let him move back in, and now he kept trying to rape me! My mind was whirling with these thoughts that refused to travel to my mouth. If only she had paid attention to me, she would have known. I always told myself that. She said she would make an appointment to start my counseling again. Yet what was counseling going to do for me at this point? I didn't need that type of help. I just ignored her and walked away as usual. Whenever I got in trouble, my mom still thought that was the solution for me. I was so sick of that.

Later, there was no sign of my Uncle James, so when I returned to fix my plate, I asked my mom where he was. She said she didn't know, so I hoped he didn't come home. Maybe I wouldn't be terrified of going to sleep. After eating, I watched TV on the couch, and my mom left for work. I tried to stay up as long as possible to watch and see if Uncle James would come home. I was getting so sleepy, but I tried to keep my eyes open.

Trying to numb the worry, I entered the kitchen to get myself some E&J liquor that Johnny had left. I would always drink every time he left, and he never knew. I took a few sips and got a little dizzy. I went upstairs to my room, and I felt kind of woozy. I just wanted to feel relaxed. When I got up the stairs, I put on my nightgown and fell straight to my bed. I think I fell straight asleep. Finally, I was sleeping so well and peacefully.

Then everything changed. All of a sudden, my mouth was covered. I popped my eyes open, and it was my Uncle James. His hands were so strong it felt like I was suffocating. He was leaning on the side of my bed, standing naked with a towel around him. I screamed, but no one was home to hear me. He got on top of me and pushed me under him. It hurt so much—oh my God, it hurt. He was still so strong, just like he was when I was a little girl. My body became paralyzed from terror.

Then, with so much force, he shoved his penis inside me. I felt it throughout my entire body. He started humping me, telling me that I still felt so good to him, just like I used to.

Desperate to escape, I kept trying to fight, to get him off of me, but I just didn't have the strength. I started begging him to stop, but he wouldn't. Instead, he just told me that he knew I liked it. I hated it. The truth was, it was horrifying and always excruciatingly painful.

I just lay there and started to dissociate, slipping into another world like I did as a child. I could hear him moaning loudly and felt him kissing me. His sweat dripped on me like rain. I felt so nasty, like a piece of trash being thrown away. He stopped, gripped my arms tightly, and then turned me over and raped me anally.

Afterward, I wanted to die. I just wanted him to kill me then. My throat wouldn't stop screaming. The pain kept growing. I already felt like I was dying anyway.

I asked him why he was doing this to me.

He said, "I love you." — the same answer as always.

He put his hand on the back of my head so my face was pressed down on the pillow. I struggled to get up from the pillow for air; I felt out of breath and lightheaded.

In that moment, I remember praying inside my head, asking God to make him stop. I begged God to help me. I just wanted it to end. I thought I would never be at this point again in my life. Why was he doing the same thing to me again? I was being raped by my uncle again, an experience I never wanted to happen again. When he moved out the first time, I thought I was free from this hurt.

Even after he stopped, I still felt him inside of me, moving back and forth. He moaned really loudly, and then I felt something really warm inside. That was when he finally stopped and got up. He whispered in my ear and told me not to tell anyone, saying that I would keep this secret because no one would believe me. He told me I was still his favorite niece. I lay there on my bed, my body in excruciating pain but simultaneously so numb. I was in so much pain that I couldn't even move.

Afterwards, I asked myself why I let my Uncle James rape me again. I shouldn't have drunk that liquor. Maybe I would have been more alert. Perhaps I should've locked my bedroom door. I always kept my guard up. I was smarter than this. I thought that since I was older now, I could have fought him off. I'm not that little girl anymore. I felt so stupid that it had happened to me. A thousand things were racing in my mind about how I could have prevented this.

I was confused and scared, and I blamed myself. I didn't know what else to do. I couldn't tell anyone because I was ashamed.

I was too scared to leave my room. I was afraid my uncle would come back and rape me again. I was terrified of him. He was a horrible monster. After the attack, I had to get up and clean myself off; I felt disgusting. I felt so sticky and nasty down there and wanted to wash everything away. I went to the bathroom and was in too much pain to even use the toilet. I could hardly wipe myself, and when I did, there was blood.

Seeing the blood triggered me. I burst into tears not even a moment later, holding my stomach and rocking myself. The pain felt like I was being stabbed; I couldn't really explain it well. I thought that maybe if I sat there long enough, the pain would ease a bit. I was able to get up and turn the shower on. When I got in, I scrubbed my body until I felt like I was scrubbing my skin off. But I couldn't take the dirtiness away that I was feeling. I wanted to erase it all, especially from my mind.

I stayed in the shower for a very long time. I kept telling myself, This isn't real. I had to repeat that over and over: This isn't real. I didn't want to accept it; I wanted it to disappear. I screamed loudly, and it felt like I was losing my mind. I couldn't get him out of my head. I could still hear his voice, telling me all those disgusting things while lying on top of me. I thought I was going insane. I think I had a mental breakdown that night. I had never felt so far from sanity before. I was only 17 and still going through so much stuff. I had taken so much as a kid and survived, my body staying alive like a battery that never went dead.

Afterward, I sat on the toilet, looking for a razor. I wanted to cut myself; I was ready to die for real. My mom usually kept a razor in the bathroom, but for some reason, it wasn't there. Maybe this was God's way of telling me I needed to live. I just sat there staring into the silence that surrounded me.

I got up to get some Tylenol out of the medicine cabinet and doped myself up with it. I was still in pain, and it made me so afraid. I went into my room and curled up into a ball, rocking myself and crying the entire time. I was hoping it would all end soon. I never told anyone about what happened to me that night. I buried that secret inside me for years. He put me through so much that my life was shattered all over again. I was still stuck with emptiness, trying to find my way.

For years, throughout my life, I had been living in shame. The shame built up so much inside. I didn't know how to release it. I was broken. I wanted my mother's love. My Uncle James and Michael had hurt me, and I had no one else to turn to. Everyone around me let me down. It still hurts to this day to even think about the pain. Even so, I was strong—I kept fighting and surviving it all.

CHAPTER 12

I didn't care about life anymore. I didn't care what would happen to me either. Life felt empty. I had no worth, no purpose, and no hope. I started to believe that nothing would ever get better for me. I considered myself already dead. Being raped by Uncle James again tore my soul into pieces. I don't think people truly understand the lasting scars those events left on me. I felt like damaged goods. I tried so hard to survive what happened. I would do my best to push back all the pain, but I couldn't get it out of my mind.

The trauma had buried itself so deep in my brain. The flashbacks were immediate and brutal whenever I closed my eyes. I would see him, and the nightmares would start all over again. I could still hear his voice telling me how sweet I was, how I wanted it, how I liked it. I would be no good to anyone. I could still feel him all over my body. I was broken into pieces that I could never put back together again.

I was drowning in this enormous secret. I started running from my pain. I felt like I would never be set free from him as long as he was living there. All I wanted was to escape. I thought that was the only way out for me.

I remember calling Michael. At that point, I really didn't care. I knew he had hurt me before, but I was already hurting. I was used to being controlled and manipulated. Maybe going back to my old ways would ease my pain. Somehow in my mind, I thought I would feel free.

He was happy to hear from me. The first thing I told him was to come get me. I got ready and put on a tight red dress. I had to be quick; I didn't want my mom to come home and catch me like that. She was at the casino, one of her favorite places. I did my usual and went to the corner to wait for Michael. He arrived fast, and I jumped in as quickly as possible. He said, "Dang baby, are you that happy to see me?" I was just trying not to let anyone notice me. He leaned over to kiss me. I made a strange face; I didn't like it, but I played it off. He said we were going to have some fun.

We pulled up at a big brick house that looked like a mansion. Inside it was huge—the floors were wooden and shiny. I couldn't believe it. I had never seen a house so big. The music was loud. I saw about three men and a few women dancing for them.

This one guy kept watching me while I stood against the wall. Michael was at the liquor counter, fixing a drink. He came over, handed me one, and I started drinking. After a few sips, I felt lighter—almost free.

Michael said, "Let me see you dance. Come on, baby, dance for me a little." I laughed, but he stayed serious. I let the music move me and began to dance.

Then Michael pointed to the man who had been staring at me earlier. He told me to go dance for him. I felt nervous, but I went along—I didn't want to make him mad.

When I reached the man, he told me I was beautiful. "Don't be shy," he said. "Just feel the music." He pulled me close and told me to turn around. He said I had a nice body and looked good in my dress. I started moving my body in front of him.

When I looked back, Michael was gone. I kept dancing, trying to play along, when the man told me to take off my dress. I froze. He wanted me to expose myself in a room full of people. I took another sip of liquor, forced myself forward, and slid my dress down slowly.

Then he told me to take off my bra. That made me even more nervous. I had been with strangers before, but this felt different. It felt wrong. Still, I did it. He told me to keep dancing and said how nice I looked.

Michael came back, put his hands on my shoulders, and whispered that I should show the man a good time. I knew what that meant. Michael's control over me was always there.

So I kept dancing. The man pulled me onto his lap, and I felt his hard penis pressing against me. I jumped up quickly, but he pulled me back down. He grabbed my breast hard, telling me I was young and tender. I forced myself to keep moving, wondering how long it would last. His heavy breathing made me sick.

I tried to block it out by focusing on the music. The more I danced, the more my mind drifted away. I must have danced for about an hour, though I can't say for sure.

When it ended, he reached into his pocket and handed me around $100. My eyes got wide. After all that, it felt like easy money. I told myself it wasn't so bad—at least sex wasn't involved.

That was the first time I started dancing for money. Afterward, Michael came over, grabbed my hand, and said, "I have another job for you." I grabbed my bra, trying to put it back on, but Michael told me I didn't need it.

He led me to another guy in the room with large muscles. He was sitting on a gray couch. When I got over there, he told me I looked good and that my body was thick and juicy. He wanted me to dance for him.

I climbed onto his lap and started dancing, turning around and moving to the beat. This time, I had gotten the hang of it from the first dance. It felt smoother, easier. I was learning fast, and the money was going to be good. For the first time, I felt powerful because I was the one controlling it.

He said, "Let's go somewhere else. I want you private."

We walked down a long hallway lined with pictures. At the end was a bathroom with a faint blue light. We went inside. My stomach tightened—I already knew where this was leading.

I tried to back away, saying, "I'm just gonna go back up to the front."

He replied, "Come on, I'm paying you, baby. Let's just go in here for a minute."

But that "minute" turned into something more. He walked over to the sink, unzipped his pants, and pulled out his penis. It looked big, and I froze, wishing I wasn't there. All I wanted to do was dance.

He started touching himself and then grabbed my head, forcing me to kneel. He told me to put my mouth on it, and I did. It was disgusting, and I almost choked. He held my head tight and wouldn't let me go. I took my mind somewhere else—like I always did—and gave this total stranger a blow job in the bathroom.

I was tired and wished he would hurry up. All I could hear was his moaning, telling me how good it was.

As soon as he finished, I ran to the sink and washed out my mouth. I even grabbed a bar of soap—nasty as it was—because I had to get that taste out.

He told me I was nice again and handed me $150 just for the blow job. In my mind, I thought it was supposed to be sex included, but I was glad it hadn't gone that far.

When he left the bathroom, I stood there for a moment, staring at myself in the mirror, thinking, What are you doing?

After that night, everything inside me felt frayed and thin. I had a guilty conscience, but it seemed like this was all I was worth and all I was ever good at. This is how men looked at me. I wanted to cry, but I held it in. I could do the easy dancing, but I hated when it turned into sex. I made about $250. I looked for Michael and saw him standing at the table, smoking. I told him I was ready to go home. I was exhausted and sleepy. He said to give him a minute, so I went and sat down.

After a short while, he came over and said, "Let's go." The music was still playing, and more people had gathered in the house. We climbed into his truck and drove off. He asked how I liked it. I just said it was okay. He told me I had made good money that night. Every time I went out with him, it was about money, drinking, and weed. We never did anything normal. I guess that was part of him being my pimp, even though he'd once been my boyfriend.

When we reached my street, I had him pull up halfway to my house because I was too tired to walk. My mom still wasn't home, which felt like a small relief.

I stepped onto the porch and opened the door. Right before the steps, Uncle James was there. He asked where I had been. I said nothing; I froze. He grabbed my arm and asked if I had told anyone about the other day. I told him no and pulled my arm away. He told me he was moving out soon and that he would miss me. I was glad to hear he was leaving again. I snatched my arm free, ran upstairs, and locked my door. I pushed my desk against it for extra protection.

Inside my room, panic and dread rushed through me. He yelled for me to come back down, but I couldn't. All I could think was, What if he rapes me again? I couldn't let that happen. I couldn't wait to move out again. I wanted to be normal and not be afraid. I wanted peace. Even after he first moved out, the memories stayed with me, and life felt like total hell. It was a life I never wanted. My shame was something I couldn't tell anyone about. I felt upside down and didn't know where to turn. I was hopeless. Looking back, sometimes I can't believe what happened. My uncle destroyed me and broke my soul.

When you're abused, it makes you feel like you have nothing. I found myself doing things a teenager should never have to do.

I learned to hide everything so well that I never got caught. I was good at surviving, but I felt like a no-good teen nobody would want. I lived with no hope, feeling worthless, using my body to get what I needed. It hurt, but I grew numb. My soul kept crying out for help. I finally broke down in my room because I couldn't take it any longer. My head felt like it would explode. It was unbearably painful to carry all of it alone. I still couldn't understand why the abuse had to happen to me.

I was emotionally drained. I carried so much inside my head that I wanted to release it. I was fighting to learn how to get it out of my mind. I had carried this shame and hurt since I was seven years old. That was when I first endured what my uncle did to me. He trapped me and molded my mind not to ever tell anyone. He was like a buried secret deep within my soul, waiting to get out.

As I grew older, I was a teenager, but that little girl was still buried inside. I was living her life, bound by the secret I carried. She was screaming to get out. She was still hurt. She was still sad. And she was still alone. She felt she had no one to rescue her.

Most of all, she wanted to be saved by her mother. She hoped and prayed each day that her mother would come and take away all the pain. She longed for her to believe her, to make the monster go away, and to never let him return. That was her biggest hope and dream. Even as I held on, I hoped one day it would come true.

CHAPTER 13

After months of carrying the weight alone, I reached a point where the hiding no longer helped. I was dealing with a life sentence of the pain of guilt and shame. I had held my pain in for so long. Instead of getting angry when people took advantage of me, I took the blame; even though it wasn't my fault, I kept quiet. The world I was living in became darker and darker. Many nights, I didn't want to dance but did whatever I had to do to make money. I needed to make enough money. I had big plans to run away.

I dreamed about New York—the place I had always wanted to go. I never really planned it out; I just wanted to get away as far as I could. I wanted to get away from Uncle James. He wasn't moving out fast enough. I wanted him to disappear. Still, seeing him constantly brought on more pain and deeper depression. The depression pushed me to try to end my life more than once.

Many days after school, I would lock myself in my room and stare at the wall. The flashbacks in my head came faster and faster. Sometimes it was hard to breathe; my heart would pound so hard it felt like it might explode. I hated that awful feeling. I would still feel like that child gasping for air. As a teenager, I still wondered why God allowed me to endure the most agonizing pain. Why did it have to be me? I would repeat that in my head often.

I knew the things I was doing were wrong. I was covering up the hurt and pain because I didn't know how to deal with it or with myself. The truth is you can't cover up trauma. It only keeps you in a dark place; the bad memories will always exist. Every time I pushed them away, they resurfaced. There was a constant war inside me—the battle I feared most. I wanted to be real for once. I wanted to shout so loud that my voice would be heard; I wanted to scream it to the mountains.

Shame was a heavy burden that followed me everywhere. I was afraid of what people would think, so I would shrink back and bury my feelings even deeper. The pressure built up into a quiet rage; I stayed silent, pretending things were fine. In the back of my mind, I hoped someone would see the real me I had buried deep in my soul. I wanted someone to tell her, "It's okay — you don't have to hide the pain anymore. You can come out; it's going to be okay. I'm here to help you get through this."

When will my truth ever begin? That question lingered in my heart, especially on the nights when Michael called. One evening, I remember Michael calling me to go do this job. It wasn't a job to dance; it was a sexual job. I was hesitant about doing it, but I said yes just like I always did. I didn't care; I just needed the money. I also knew that if I said no, he would be mad.

I was always afraid of Michael. I never knew which way he would come at me. Sometimes, he could be very nice, and I would accept it. I didn't know any better; I just wanted to feel love. Deep down inside, he really wasn't any good for me, but I was so used to being controlled that I had developed low self-esteem.

I had no self-love because of the abuse I took from my uncle. I thought that when a man told me something, I had to do what he said. I guess that's why I didn't want to go. It wasn't ever a good feeling. I took a lot—whether it was getting hit or roughed up during sex. I just got used to it after so many times. Just like when I was a little girl, I was always treated like some type of object or dog. The men were disgusting to me, and even the attractive ones didn't turn me on.

When Michael came to pick me up, he told me this job was worth a lot of money. My eyes got big, but in the back of my head, I felt uneasy about doing it. My body was completely numb; it was a feeling

I had never had before. It wasn't a nervous feeling, because I had gotten used to it. I had trained my mind to go through with these jobs.

We pulled up to a motel near downtown Detroit. The green lights were flashing on the sign, and it was dark. We got out of his truck and went inside. The smell was awful—like something had died. I held my breath; I didn't like it. Michael told the man at the counter who he was there to see. The room was upstairs, and the walls were filthy. The paint was peeling, and I saw a roach crawling on one of the doors we walked past. My stomach turned instantly, and I wanted to throw up.

We walked up to a room with a small hole in the door. Michael said it looked like a bullet hole. When he opened the door, there was a man inside. His eyes were dark, and he was very tall. He kept staring at me, smiling. I heard Michael telling him it was for the whole job—I knew what that meant. Michael walked away, kissed me on the cheek, and told me he would be back. That was always his charming way of buttering me up. I knew his scheming ways; he was never up to any good. Still, I dealt with him, because I had no choice.

As often as he hurt me and put me in dangerous situations, I was lost and couldn't find my way out. It was his way of giving me the go-ahead just because I was getting paid. When the door closed, it echoed in my head like a warning I couldn't escape. I stood there and heard the man tell me to come over. He never told me his name. I walked slowly toward him.

He told me I had a nice body and instantly started kissing me. His breath was hot, and it felt like he was trying to shove his tongue in my mouth. I hated it so much; it reminded me of when my uncle would kiss me—sweaty, forceful, with liquor on his breath.

I didn't like it, so I pushed him away with my hand. Suddenly, he pulled out a knife and told me I was going to give him what he wanted—no time for games. I pleaded with him, saying he didn't have to do that. I was so scared my body was trembling. He ordered me to take my clothes off. Still shaking, I looked around the room, desperate for a way out.

I started moving toward the door, but he grabbed me and yanked me back toward the bed. He ripped my shirt off while I kept begging, "please." Then he threw me to the floor. He started choking me, and I couldn't breathe. I kicked and screamed, fighting to get up. He tried to pull my shorts down, but I kept kicking. His hands were all over me, and he kept saying he would "show me a good time."

I clawed at his face, digging my nails deep into his skin. That night I felt like I had powers. I knew what this was leading to, and I was afraid, but I couldn't let anyone else rape me again. I kept fighting him off. When I saw him reaching for the knife, I kicked him hard between the legs. He cursed, calling me a bitch, while clutching himself and still trying to grab me.

I got up and ran out of the room as fast as I could. Tears streamed down my face as I ran down the hall, half-naked with no shirt on. I didn't care—I was terrified.

When I got outside, Michael was standing by the car, smoking a cigarette. He looked at me and yelled, "What the hell happened? Why are you running?" I cried, telling him that man was crazy, that he had a knife and tried to force himself on me.

Michael grabbed me by the arm and told me to get in the car. He was furious, shouting, "I can't believe you! You messed up some really good money tonight." But this time, I didn't care at all. I was tired of being abused and hurt by men. I couldn't take it anymore. I realized I was risking my life every night—having sex with strangers, with no protection.

After that night, something inside me finally shifted. I knew deep down that I wanted to be free from all of it. That explained why I had been so hesitant to go—my mind and body were screaming that I was worth more than this. I kept telling myself I needed to break free, because there was no telling how it might have ended if I hadn't fought back. That man literally tried to choke me to death and pulled a knife on me.

In the midst of that terror, I didn't know how I was going to get away from Michael. He was more than just my boyfriend; he was acting like a pimp. After I got into the car, Michael slapped me hard. He yelled, "You're gonna pay for this. You're acting like a little girl now, see?" I cried, telling him I was sorry, but I couldn't do it anymore. He demanded, "What do you mean?" and then grabbed my hair, yanking it so hard I screamed. I begged him to stop, telling him it hurt. He just repeated himself, angrier than ever.

The atmosphere inside that car was terrifying. He sped down the street, driving faster than he ever had before. I thought we were going to crash. He was acting so strange, and I was terrified. I begged him over and over to please take me home.

Finally, he pulled up to my street. I didn't even say goodbye; I was just relieved to be home—even though home had never felt like a safe place. I was shaken to my core; this had been one of the craziest nights of my life. I got out of the car, and he burned rubber as he sped off. All I could think about was getting inside, taking a shower, and collapsing in bed.

As I approached the house, I saw that my mom was home. Fear gripped me again—I hoped she would already be asleep. But when I stepped inside, Uncle James was sitting at the table, eating and drinking his beer as if he owned the place. My chest tightened. I ran upstairs quickly, saw my mom's door was closed, and locked myself in my room. I shoved my desk against the door for extra protection.

Standing in front of the mirror, I broke down crying and started talking to myself, asking, "Why are you doing this?" Deep in my heart, I knew I needed to release the shame and hurt soon. Part of me believed no one would ever believe me, and that guilt was eating my soul alive.

I stared at my reflection and noticed a small red mark on my neck from when the man at the motel had grabbed me. I promised myself I would hide it—just like I hid all the other scars—so no one would ever know. Even the bruises from being roughed up didn't compare to the scars left by being sexually abused.

The weight of it all pressed against my chest, crushing me. I had felt that pain often but never understood what it was. Later, I would learn it was anxiety—something I was finally diagnosed with when I started seeing my therapist.

I remember the first day I started seeing my therapist. I was almost eighteen. She was a white lady with reddish hair and freckles on her face. Her name was Mary. The first session my mom took me to was on the northeast side. The lobby was painted gray with brown chairs. Mary's office was white, and she had a black desk with a vase of red flowers. I was sitting at the table. My mom was with Mary at her desk, and they were talking. Then Mary motioned for my mom to come over, and she started asking me questions. Her first question was, "Your mom says you get angry often?" She asked me to tell her a little about myself. I was afraid to say anything. I couldn't tell her what was going on. I thought I was the worst person in the world.

Mary gave my mom a look and asked if she would mind waiting out in the lobby. Of course, my mom looked a little mad—I could tell by her face. After my mom left, Mary came back to the table and told me that anything I said in her office was confidential. I didn't have to worry; she was there because she wanted to help me. She could tell I had a lot of anger bottled up inside. She was right. I wanted to scream right then and there, but I didn't trust her yet. I had a problem trusting anyone. I was afraid she would let me down. I had to feel comfortable inside before I could open up.

She started by asking me simple things—did I like school? What made me angry? Did I have any siblings? Then came the question that cut deeper: "What was it like growing up?" Something had to have made me so angry. My throat tightened with a big knot. My eyes went watery, and I fought to hold the tears back. I couldn't let one fall. My voice felt stuck. I just sat there, and she said, "So tell me the things you like to do." I told her I liked to write in my journal when I was sad. I told her I liked doing hair, too. That was all I could manage. I couldn't tell her about the life I was living behind closed doors—I pretended I was perfect. But I was living a big, fat lie under the weight of a huge secret. I heard the clock beep; time was up. She said she would see me next week.

She seemed nice. Maybe I could trust her one day. On the drive home, my mom asked what they had talked about. I said, "She asked why I was angry—something about school." My mom snapped, "You don't go telling her my business either." I just looked at her and couldn't say a word. I wanted her to be there for me.

I continued therapy once a week with Mary, and I began to talk a little more each time. Sometimes we played card games; she made the sessions comfortable. Then she started asking me to write out my feelings. The more I wrote, the more I opened up on the page. She never asked to read my journal; she said it was for me to know, and whenever I wanted to talk about it, I could. She never pushed; she let things move at my pace until I was ready.

Slowly, I started to build confidence. I could talk a little about school or about how I felt when my mom was home. Mary always listened. She told me she cared about my feelings and never tried to tear me down. She kept telling me I was safe—words I had been craving to hear.

One day I wasn't having a good night. I couldn't sleep; paranoia rose up again. I woke up sweating so badly I could hardly breathe. In the dream, I was a little girl running from my uncle, trying to find somewhere to hide so he wouldn't find me. No matter where I went, he would appear. I woke up screaming and checked that my door was locked. I had to remind myself he had finally moved out—he left not long after I started therapy with Mary. I felt a little free, but the nightmares kept coming.

That same day I had a session, and I sat in the lobby feeling down from the rough night. When Mary came out and called my name, I was in a daze. She called again, and I looked up. She smiled and told me to come back. I stood and followed her into the room, my head bowed but a fragile hope beginning to stir.

I'm looking down at the squares on the carpet and counting them. When we got to her office, I just flopped down onto her black couch. I grabbed a pillow from the couch and held it as tight as I could. I wanted to put it over my face and scream; I needed to lash out. She asked if I was OK. I sat there, mute. Then I spoke softly and said, "Yes, I'm okay."

She said, "I don't think so; you look very sad. Do you want to talk about it?" I told her I couldn't. I was scared. She said I didn't have to be; it was okay. I looked up at her and started crying. She asked, "Why are you crying, honey?" I said, "I don't know — I'm just scared."

In the back of my mind I kept worrying that if I told Mary this big secret, she would do to me what my middle-school teacher did—let me down. I had always kept that fear. After I had told my teacher about my uncle and how she did nothing to help me, I didn't know whether I could trust Mary. I was really afraid of breaking down—what would happen to me then?

How would my family react? What would my mom think? People seemed to think I was just a bad seed. I was so ashamed. When would this guilt ever end? All I knew was I was hurting deep inside. It felt like a hole burning in my heart, crushing me—holding everything: the abuse from my uncle, the rape, Michael abusing me, and being forced to sleep with those men.

Everything felt overwhelming; I had taken so much in my years of growing up. I held on to it all in a little secret box of shame that was constantly overflowing.

CHAPTER 14

After carrying my secret for so long, the weight became unbearable, and I finally reached the point where I could no longer keep it inside.

I struggled so much that I did not think I could heal. I didn't know where to begin, and I felt completely lost. I had kept it hidden for so long that it had become my everyday life. I was still convinced I could never tell anyone what had happened to me. Over time, I began to believe my struggles were simply a part of who I was. Still, I sat on Mary's couch, terrified to tell her. Every session felt the same. My heart raced, a knot tightened in my throat, and I knew I had to tell her how much this was hurting me. I looked up at her as she wrote at her desk. I was so nervous that the shame consumed me inside. I remember my legs started shaking.

I said to Mary, "There is something I have to tell you. I'm so scared; I have been carrying this secret."

She said, "Go ahead, hon — what secret?"

A tear rolled down my face. She got up to get me some Kleenex, and my legs began shaking faster, my heart pounding harder and harder.

Suddenly, "I blurted out fast, my uncle touched me." Then I said it again.

"My uncle used to touch me. He used to have sex with me."

Just saying those words choked me up. The heaviness in my

throat felt tighter. I knew I had mentioned it before to Margo and my previous counselor; that always happened when the words came out of my mouth. I could see her eyes grow really wide, and she came over to the couch and sat beside me. I was crying, rocking back and forth, holding my head. It felt like my head was about to explode. Memories were racing, and I started having flashbacks of everything. I could barely breathe. I was having an anxiety attack. She held me, whispering it would be ok. She kept saying she was sorry this happened to me. She got up and got me a glass of water. She had one of those little water machines in her office. I'm thinking in my head; please believe me. When she got back to the couch, it was like I couldn't stop crying. All I wanted was to be free. She sat back down and said "Look at me." I slowly held my head up. She put her hands on my shoulders. I remembered this so much it's like I was back at that very moment. She said, "You don't have to be afraid anymore; it was not your fault. What your uncle did to you was horrible. You were just a little girl; you didn't deserve that. You don't have to live with that secret anymore. I'm here. I BELIEVE YOU."

I always wanted someone to believe me. Those words felt like magic. Her gentle voice was so soothing I felt a little relief. For many years I felt so powerless I thought I could not tell my secret. I had buried it so deep. But I realized that someone out there cared about me. The abuse always made me feel worthless. My uncle made me believe I was ruined. I was crazy. He made me feel no one would ever believe me. He blamed me and made it look like it was my fault. All along, he was protecting himself. If I told someone, they would blame me. It was like self-pity I put upon myself. But I was capable of telling someone. It was up to me to allow myself to tell about my abuse. How could I allow myself to open up? Being abused destroyed me and my boundaries. I had no power over my life; it was taken away. My sexual abuse happened to me regularly, and I had to survive it through my mind. Some days I would apologize to myself like I did something wrong. My uncle made me feel that way. The voice that I kept silent became stronger and stronger.

Each time I saw Mary, I was able to hear my voice. I was able to talk about what happened to me, and even the fear in me was slowly fading away.

On this particular day, I came home from school and had a session with Mary. My therapy sessions were usually scheduled after school. Sometimes I would catch a cab when I didn't have a ride because I didn't drive.

When I got to the center, I waited in the lobby. Mary was taking a little longer than usual, and I started getting nervous, thinking she wouldn't come out and get me. I always got nervous when I thought I was being disappointed. I looked at the black clock on the wall; it was fifteen minutes past my time. My session was supposed to start at 5:00 p.m.

Finally, I looked down the hall and saw her door open. She was walking a teenage boy out. Then she called me back, and she smiled. What a relief—I had feared she had let me down.

When we got into her office, I sat down. The first thing she said to me was, "I want to try something different with you today. Can you trust me?" I was a little hesitant. I looked up and said, "Yes."

Then she said, "I would like for you to talk about your abuse."

I bucked my eyes open wide! I had told her bits and pieces about what happened with my uncle, but I never really talked about it in full. Feeling the pain was just too overwhelming for me. The memories were too traumatizing, and I didn't want to think about it.

So, when she asked me, I got really scared. But I told myself I had to give it a try. After all, how was I supposed to heal if I never really expressed my emotions? The ones that were hurting me inside. I never got the chance to express my feelings to anyone. I was always carrying shame.

She asked me how old I was when it began.

I told her I was seven years old. I remember her saying, "You were so young. You were just a little girl; that's so hurtful." All I could do was sit there and see the hurt on her face. I could tell she really cared. I just started talking. I told her it happened mostly when he babysat me, at night while everyone was asleep. Those memories were so awful—I hated remembering everything: the smell of liquor on his breath, his heavy breathing, his hands all over me.

I told her I would always pray for him to stop, but my prayers were never answered. He threatened me not to tell anyone. I started crying, and I couldn't catch my breath. The hurt was eating me up inside. Still, I was determined not to give up. I needed to release this.

Yet I could never talk about the sexual details. That was the hardest part. It was so painful; I felt ashamed and continued blaming myself. I had developed negative feelings for letting him do that to me. I went through so much day after day, night after night, and I let him hurt me like that. It was disgusting that I had tolerated it. Just thinking about it made me feel sick.

The self-blame stayed with me, and my self-worth was something I had to face. This happens often with survivors—we blame ourselves, thinking we allowed it to happen. But when abusers hurt you, they make it seem like it's your fault. They twist it into punishment, as if you did something wrong. They know how to manipulate your mind because they hold power and control over you.

They make you believe they love you—as if this is how they show it. And so, they think it's okay, convincing themselves it's normal while using your pain against you.

They see you hurting and take advantage of a vulnerable child. That was me. My uncle knew that whenever I was alone with him, he used that against me. He groomed me for his sexual needs right from the start. From the day he moved in, he found ways to get whatever he wanted. He knew my mom worked, and that I had no protection.

He took advantage of that. He also knew my mom loved him so much. When he was nice to her, she wouldn't pay any attention to me.

He fed me lies to protect himself, saying things like, "If you love me, you will let me." Those are the ways uncles take advantage. He told me things to prevent anyone from finding out and to keep me from telling.

When I told Mary my truth, facing it was very painful, but it was healing for me. Beneath all that pain, I found the sweet, loving child I once was—before my uncle came into my life and made it hell. I remembered her so clearly—her funny smile and how joyful she used to be.

I discovered myself again. I realized I didn't have to keep dealing with Michael—I needed to deal with my past and finally be free from that abuse. I didn't need to keep giving my body away; I needed to stop putting myself in those dangerous situations. I didn't deserve to live that way. I had to get it out of my mind. Just because your uncle destroyed your life, you don't have to keep destroying yourself.

When I discovered this, it became such a beautiful thing. I knew I could live free.

Mary truly listened to me, and in her listening, she gave me hope. I talked about my abuse, and with each session, I began to reclaim my life. I never gave up on going to therapy because I had finally found a safe place. That safe space allowed me to grow more comfortable, little by little.

I learned that allowing myself to feel safe and set boundaries helped me open up more about my pain. I realized I didn't have to keep the wall up that I had built over the years. It was okay to release it.

As I opened up, I became gentler with myself, and the self-blame started to fade away. The anger I had carried for so long felt like it was never even there. With each step, I moved closer toward healing.

It was as if I had finally given myself permission to live. For the first time, I felt safe inside. It was a feeling I couldn't fully explain—only that it was real, and it was mine. I finally trusted myself to let go of all that fear and shame.

CHAPTER 15

Just when I thought I was beginning to find a rhythm in my healing, life shifted again. My therapist left, and her departure was not just a goodbye—it felt like the reopening of an old wound. I felt as though my world had collapsed. I would wake up in the middle of the night, my heart pounding heavily from the trauma of how my uncle had violated me. When my therapist left, I was hollow. I had opened up to her and thought she would be there for me. I truly believed she would stay, only to find myself abandoned. Perhaps she assumed I would find another person to open up to, but that was not how I felt.

Opening up to her after finally trusting someone again had been a personal decision that had dragged on for years after my uncle violated me. It was a matter of finding peace, a matter of seeking comfort. I felt like I had my head trapped between two firmly joined irons, and Niagara Falls poured over me—I was drowning. It wasn't that I had recovered from the trauma of the violation, but my therapist's leaving overwhelmed me.

Where would I begin? Could I continue, and could I move forward? These were the questions that occasionally popped into my mind. I had no answers. Still, I would remember my sessions with her and how she would tell me that all would be well. She said it was normal for me to be worried, anxious, angry with others, and to struggle with trusting again. I remember how she looked into my eyes and said, *"It's okay; I'm right here."* In the process of hearing about what happened between my uncle and me, she helped me build small pieces of confidence in myself. The trauma held me tight like a mother holding her only child. I was devastated. My uncle had made it seem as if he did me a favor that no one must know about. At a tender age, I had to figure things out.

Struggling with the trauma, I was always fighting within myself, wondering if anyone would ever believe me. He didn't realize how hurt I was and how broken I had become.

Then my therapist arrived in my life: someone who would listen, hold, and tell me things would improve with time. I followed her guidance and trusted everything she told me. She led me through sessions and started getting me out of the hole. I was peeling away the shell that covered me—the self-pain inside me—but then she left. Her leaving knocked me off balance and shattered my fragile hope. I began to wonder if there would ever be change, or if the world was made only for my suffering. I asked myself whether there was anything in the world beyond pain, agony, and constant rejection.

It boiled inside me. I accepted that perhaps the world was not made for comfort but for struggle. I felt like I was drowning; someone would take my hand and begin to pull me up, and then they would let go—and I would be left sinking again into unknown, deep waters.

After my therapist left, I tried to hold myself together, but the cracks only grew wider. I carried her absence like a weight, and even in the smallest moments of daily life, I felt it pressing down. It was during one of those ordinary school days, when the teachers had just finished their weekly meeting, that another memory was triggered—one I had buried deep but could not escape.

I remember that afternoon clearly. Mr. Thomas, the Civic Studies teacher, was one of my favorite teachers. He had just entered our class, and I looked up, catching his presence as he walked in.

He was dressed in a dark suit with brown snakeskin leather shoes laced neatly. The watch on his wrist shone bright like diamonds, but it didn't outshine his smiling face. He would always smile in the

The Healing Wound

classroom, and his smile followed him wherever he moved. Whether it was morning or afternoon, Mr. Thomas's smile never seemed to fade. It wasn't regulated by time—it was simply who he was.

As he entered the classroom, students began preparing for the debate question he had given us in the last class. He had asked us to compare military rule with civil rule and choose a side to support. I had stayed up the night before reading about military rule in Africa. Whether I was fully prepared for the contest or not didn't matter—I just wanted to prove I was smart. Some students sometimes called me dumb, and I wanted to prove them wrong.

But then, in an instant, my focus shifted. As I watched Mr. Thomas, the sight of his well-trimmed mustache reminded me of something I had long tried to bury. A memory rose up without warning, dragging me back into a darker place.

Suddenly, I was no longer in the classroom. I was back in the past—back in the grip of my uncle. I remembered how he held me and brushed his mustache over my chest. The memory of his harsh, monster-like voice filled my ears again. His words echoed: dirty whispers, lies wrapped in manipulation. *"You're no good… I have to take good care of you. I love you."*

In that moment, I couldn't think clearly. My mind was lost. I asked myself if this was the "care" he thought I needed, or if there was some twisted version of love that I had yet to understand. I didn't know what to think. I was confused.

The pain was so real, and I didn't fully realize how wrong it all was until I grew older, in my late teens. That's when the memories became sharper, clearer. I started remembering more of what had happened, and each detail cut into me like glass.

I never spoke of it to anyone. Yet, I could never forget how layered his mustache was—each strand brushing against me, each one carrying a memory of pain. I was helpless. I was lost.

Back in the classroom, I snapped back to reality to see my classmate, Jason Barley — a Hispanic boy with short black hair — deliver his speech on military rule while Mr. Thomas turned to me and asked me to name three features of military rule. I didn't even notice he had pointed at me until a fellow student touched my arm. The present had caught up with me. Not that I hadn't read about military rule the night before — I had — but Mr. Thomas's mustache had dragged me back into my uncle's world. I had to find my way back when he called on me to answer.

My mind went blank. A girl named Robin nudged me, but words failed me; I couldn't get them out. My mouth felt shut, my voice gone. It reminded me of being a little girl—silenced and small. Not that I didn't understand that military rule is characterized by certain features; I did. I knew military rule existed in different countries, but I couldn't speak the answers aloud.

Mr. Thomas may have noticed I wasn't focused. He looked away from me and continued explaining why debates about military rule and civil government usually favor civilian governance. I felt wrong—disoriented and humiliated. My self-worth sank again; my self-esteem began to fray, and I felt myself coming apart.

At lunchtime, Robin came over and asked if I was all right. I told her I was fine, even though I wasn't. Could she have understood the emptiness and the long-standing pain I carried? The departure of my therapist had left a vacuum, and I didn't know if it would ever be filled. I couldn't understand why she had left me alone. I had opened up to her and expected she would stand by my side as I worked through the trauma. Instead, she left suddenly, destroying what I had been building from all those lost years.

I wanted desperately to vent my anger or to let the tears fall without shame. I needed a place to lay down the pain and the haunting memories. I had thought my therapist would be my refuge—someone who could read my mind and guide me through the darkness. Only for her to leave me in the middle of this storm. How long would this world of darkness last?

I knew I needed light. I had put my therapist on a pedestal, believing she could teach me how to trust and heal, but she left with her mind, will, and presence. Was I crazy when she left? Maybe not. The nightmares of my uncle's roughness—the way he forced himself on me—had carved scars that wouldn't fade. My mother hadn't been there to protect me, and my uncle never owned the truth.

With my therapist gone, I turned back to my diary for strength. Writing had been occasional before, but now I relied on it more. Left to bear the burden alone, I struggled to get by. I tried making new friends, but the way my therapist left had shadowed me; I feared new people would not believe me or might leave me too, dragging me deeper into shame. I wanted a place where I could shed tears without judgment, pour out my worries, and look in the mirror and tell myself, "You are somebody." I wanted to take steps toward believing in myself again.

I started writing in my journal. I would get up in the middle of the night and stand in the garden behind our house. The streets were silent, but my mind was loud. *Where do I start?* As I cried, I grabbed my diary and began to write. My thoughts raced as I put words down. I loved using my flower pen even in times of pain. What appeared on the page was a mixture of fear, pain, and struggle. I wondered if my pain would ever end. I worried that maybe my fears would fade just by writing them down. Little did I know that pouring out emotions was both difficult and courageous. Still, I needed somewhere to release my heavy heart.

I had once found comfort in my therapist, but she had left me halfway through my healing. After that, I began filling blank pages upon pages, hoping that writing would ease the emptiness inside me. Yet the more I wrote, the heavier I felt. I flipped from the back page to the front again, but instead of relief, I found more weight pressing on me. It felt like the emptiness was draining my soul, and with it came even more anxiety. My thoughts grew scattered, and I struggled to hold them together.

One Saturday morning in the summer, I woke to the sweet smell of pancakes drifting up from the kitchen. I told myself, *Let this be a happy day with my mom*. It was just the two of us, and we always seemed to clash. I went to the bathroom, brushed my teeth, washed my face, slipped on my pink housecoat, and headed downstairs.

My mom was sitting at the table drinking her coffee. I went to fix my plate, and she asked, "Did you wash your hands?" I said yes as I sat down. Then she asked how therapy was going. A lump rose in my throat. I was shocked—she hadn't even realized I wasn't in therapy anymore. That showed how little attention she paid me. I told her it was fine. I stuffed my mouth with pancakes quickly, wanting to finish before she could ask anything else. I didn't have it in me to share anything anymore. I had grown so used to dealing with things on my own. The weight pressed on me like a heavy hook around my neck, and though I longed to release my anger to her, I kept it inside.

Back in my room, I thought that maybe if I could talk—really talk—it would set me free from the bondage I carried. I imagined a guardian angel rescuing me, pulling me from the shackles of my uncle's sick mind. He wanted me to believe his violation was normal, that it was somehow love. But who would ever ask for such heartbreak? Who would ever want forced "love" and terrible suffering at such a young tender age?

Sometimes I longed for someone to hold my hands and drag me out of the murky waters I was drowning in. Each time the flood rose over me, I wanted something strong enough to wash away my struggles, my agony, and my trauma. But instead, the flood dragged me under. That drowning was the neglect of my mother, the shock of my uncle's violation, and the absence of my therapist—a therapist who had once steadied me only to suddenly leave me, like placing me on a chair and then pulling the legs away.

I opened the first pages of my diary with that flooding image still overwhelming my mind. I couldn't always identify what needed to go, but I knew something had to leave—just as a piece of me was taken the day my uncle grabbed my hands and forced me onto the couch.

Though I felt emotions within me, there were cries of pain and an urge to pour out my deepest hurt. I stopped at the middle page of my journal. I wasn't sure what that page symbolized—maybe it meant enough was enough, or maybe it was a signal to separate my life from this constant agony. I began to write on that middle page. I started with the hellish morning that followed the horrifying experience I had been forced to endure by my uncle, who had warned me not to tell anyone.

Of course, I wanted to tell someone. I wanted to talk to my mom the next morning, but I had no voice. She never paid me any attention. She didn't even look into my red eyes or see that I was suffering in pain from crying all night. She was on the phone, talking to Uncle James about the new job position she was expecting. She spoke about how she deserved it, how he used to help her around the house, and she praised him again and again. I hated it so much. The conversation went on and on with nothing about me.

I felt my uncle had trapped me in confusion, pulling me into pain on purpose. I wished my mom would hold my hands, pull me close, and ask why my eyes were teary and why I had no voice. But instead, she was far away—caught up in her job and the hope of more money. I had no problem with her wanting more money, but I felt my uncle was gaslighting me, and I didn't understand why my mom would never care for me.

So I began writing about the emptiness that came over me that morning—the pain that shattered me—and how I was forced to find my way in life at such a tender age. I wrote on the middle page that though the hurt in me rose daily and the agony of life had taken me over, I wished there could be freedom—maybe a way out of the ocean where I was drowning. Oh my gosh, I remember those exact words. These expressions came out with tears. A warm tear dropped onto the page. As it sank, it left a wet mark, and I watched it spread across the paper. I stopped. I breathed, but the tears continued. Fear stuck in me, and I began to doubt if I was right or wrong to still feel the pain. No one bothered about me, and neither did anyone care to listen to my cries.

So I wondered if maybe I didn't need to endure the pain anymore. But deep inside me, I was empty, and something inside told me my pain was genuine. I wasn't a bitter soul—I was like a fragile piece of glass that had fallen hard and shattered everywhere. Would it ever be possible to put the pieces back together again? Not even a single sign of the pain leaving me. I struggled with waiting for love from my parents, with rejection from family life, with feeling like I was crazy, with the mental detachment I began to experience at school, and with the early battles of life that had already traumatized me.

When I wrote again on the middle page, it was about the darkness that covered me on the night my uncle took my innocence. The room was lit, but darkness was all I saw. I wrote that the darkness became my life as I lay on my bed and felt something moving in and out of me. It was as if I went into another world, and in that world, I wished someone could pick me up and rescue me from the pain that held me captive.

Before I knew what was happening, tears ran down my face and I slipped into another world after that devastating experience. I struggled to find my balance. I lost consciousness even as my body remained alive—but that was no life; it felt like a child crushed by hell. My diary soon became my refuge again, just as it had when I was little and first discovered that writing about my pain helped me process it. Whenever I felt stuck, I drew closer to the pages and found strength in ink. Talking to my diary felt like conversing with a quiet superpower that sometimes soothed me and at other times seemed absent.

Still, the comfort the diary offered carried words that reached deep into my wounded spirit and urged me to keep going. My uncle's constant presence and the unexpected departure of my therapist stole any peace I might have had, and I struggled every day to move forward. It was a hard season, but the diary gave me whatever small comfort it could. I didn't know if that comfort would ever be enough, but who could say? All I wanted was a way to move on and piece my shattered heart back together—if that was even possible.

CHAPTER 16

Emptiness could not *fully* describe the leaden feeling and sudden struggle that submerged me. I tried working with my diary to regain my voice and reclaim my life. I wanted to have my life gathered again. But, like an egg splattered on the wall, the pieces remained shattered. However, a place of recovery lingered—only traveling the road was never easy, and I had no strength to journey it alone. I was desolate even though I was with my mom. Still, she never gave attention to the pain, agony, and deep inadequacy that hovered around me. I journeyed with my diary. I penned down my thoughts and wishes. I didn't take back how I wished I was never raped and wondered why it was me—only me—positioned against the world.

Now, the clouds thickened, and a rain of heaviness began to fall on me as I walked across the high-low, but seemingly only low, muddy path of life.

Would life ever be okay even once? I thought. I believed life would return to normal only to before the age of seven, when my uncle started molesting me. I shouldn't have been this battered, rejected, and left to struggle. I felt hooked by an angry fisherman who strung me along the waters of Belle Isle, without minding the life below the surface. I kept returning to the awful images of the day I was violated. I imagined the peace I would have lived if my Uncle James had never forced himself on me.

Yes, it was never wished, but it had happened, and the aftermath was pain after pain. I realized that a wish that never happened would remain a wish, and I had to move on with reality. But that was never easy. I made my journal a friend and often stained its pages with my sobbing heart.

Sometimes I would go there, writing whatever clear and unclear thoughts came to my mind. Other times, I would talk to my journal about that peace—perhaps the same one I had once seen. The description of peace became clearer when I read *The Courage to Heal* by Ellen Bass. I started doing research in my school library. I wanted to find something to help me heal on my own. I couldn't dare tell anybody else my secret again. I was still hurting from the loss of my therapist.

That book lifted me into a spectacular mindset; I saw joy among thousands of flowers at peace and felt like a bliss-bringing poet. I was overjoyed by this wander through the poet's pages because it mirrored my reality. I was wandering, lonely, along the path of life. It felt as if the world had left me behind—violated and rejected. My discovery of *The Courage to Heal* felt like an encounter, and I savored it while it lasted. I saw a family of flowers keeping their natural scent and shape, enjoying the breeze near a lake. It reminded me of my bliss before the violation erased my inner peace and threw me into battle at a tender age.

It reminded me how I had managed to live fairly well even in an uncaring environment because my mom never paid attention to me. Still, I lived well until I was abused, and then my peace poured down the drain like hot coffee into a rusty steel sink. The shrinking sound was like a blade peeling my skin—the same blade I had used twice when I tried to kill myself. I remembered those memories so clearly. I had felt that everything would be turned upside down. However, I soon returned to a steadier state of mind as the engulfing despair vaporized, as if it had never come.

The indifference of everyone around me pitched me deeper into trauma than I could have imagined. Losing concentration in class became normal as I suffered inside and outside my confines. Maintaining sanity was left entirely to me. But how could I handle a situation where everyone looked on as if all was well? It was like an earthquake.

One slightly cloudy morning I woke feeling surreal, painted in unknown colors. I didn't bother to find out why. I moved out of bed, half-conscious, reached for my journal, and checked my plans for the day. The entertainment set and TV in my room stood on one side as if they weren't part of the space. The TV's blackness didn't mean much to me. I scanned the room for the remote and tried to remember where I had left my jotter. The sound from the TV reminded me of an old record player I used to hear coming home from school in the evening, near the fireplace in the living room. The record would just blast. I never minded the sound, but that morning it struck me as something that had always been the same.

The record player sent me back into memories I couldn't quite sort out. I faintly remembered the words: *"The game of life is hard to play. I'm going to lose it anyway."* Then I connected the feeling to songs by Tupac and Notorious B.I.G., which captured the hard times the music hinted at. I snapped back to reality in the blink of an eye and returned my gaze to the TV, the song still playing while some cartoons rushed across the screen in green. I spotted the remote and flipped through channels.

While changing stations, I remembered I had left my journal on the sofa by the brown wooden door in my room. I set the remote on the table and went for the jotter. I picked up the journal and turned back to the TV just as Channel 7 News in Detroit ran a report detailing the level of rape in the country. The statistics were heavy, and it occurred to me that being among those figures was one thing—but my pain was so much greater.

I felt a deep sickness and wanted to throw up. I was dizzy and heard a steady pounding in my head. *Why has the world decided to be so cruel to a little, harmless girl like me?* I felt utterly helpless.

I felt helpless, as if I were that little girl again. I wondered why the system was not designed to protect me when I was young, why I had to carry the burden of living in hell because of my Uncle James and his violation—while he walked about unbothered, as if nothing had ever happened.

I wasn't pleased with the program I had just watched, because it turned into more of a debate filled with blame-shifting. I never thought rape could somehow be blamed on the victim, or that the prevalence of its occurrence would be blamed on victims who had not summoned enough courage to report. At the very least, victims' pain and disturbances should have been considered and respected, instead of placing an umbrella of blame on them for supposedly causing an increase in rape cases through non-disclosure.

In that moment, I felt I needed the courage to help myself and others who were trapped in the hurricane of violation at the hands of creatures who thrived on causing agony. I truly wanted to help myself out of the situation, but it was hard and painful, and I felt my strength fading as I moved along the path of life.

Later that same day, I dreamed that someone had crept into our house like a snake on a mission, its venom hidden in the cracks of the baseboard along the wall. I had just left the garden, where I had arranged the flower vases. As I moved along the balcony, I noticed that the spiced pink seat at the front wasn't properly positioned. As I tried to adjust it, I remembered how hard I had tried to focus on my studies and push the memories of my violation into the past.

I recalled settling into the school library when two girls from my class approached me. They said they had noticed I was always alone and invited me to join them so we could all read together. The invitation was not bad in itself. But as I prepared to respond, my eyes caught a set of books on the shelf labeled *The Silent Cries*. The title reminded me of my struggle—my lone fight for sanity in a world that often felt like it was falling apart.

I thanked the girls for their kind invitation but told them I wouldn't be able to join. Instead, I returned to my old, hard gray seat. I pushed the half-sofa close to the three-lined, ash-coated wall. My mom had mentioned some time back that she had swept the dirty front porch, and that memory lingered with me as I sat down again.

Whether the ash color represented what she meant or not was not my concern that day—I was busy with the watermelon I had just sliced. I picked the seeds out of the watermelon to make it taste better. I hated the seeds, but the fruit was sweet and tasty. I enjoyed every bite while my mom talked about her color choice for the new porch. Then I headed into the house.

Days later, I noticed something—or someone—moving in the living room, and I wasn't sure what it was. I heard the door slam. My mom hadn't returned yet; she had said her trip would last two days. I was supposed to be home alone. I paused and wondered what to do next. I needed to know who it was.

I moved close to the door and hesitated. I placed my hand on the knob and waited for the other side to move. The moment reminded me of an episode of *Unsolved Mysteries*—a show I used to love—where the victim's knob was dragged, and before she could call out, Jack, she was fatally shot. I prayed that this was not my situation.

I counted to fifty in my head, expecting some kind of reaction from the other side, but there was none. I opened the door but stayed back a bit to the side. I was on the Eastside of Detroit, hoping whoever it was would step into the hallway and at least show their face, but I was scared. Still, I opened the door—and no one came out.

I entered the living room only to see my Uncle James sitting on the black couch with a half-filled beer bottle. I was certain the beer wasn't from our fridge, though the meats on the table were ours. I wondered why he was there—my mom had never told me anyone was coming. I hated that he could just show up at our house at any time. My anxiety flared, and my heart began racing as if it would pound out of my chest.

I tried to make sense of what was happening, but my thoughts collapsed into a jumble. I couldn't understand why my violator would be sitting so comfortably in our home. He mumbled something; he was so drunk I couldn't hear him clearly. I saw his hand point at me and heard him tell me to sit and stop "acting funny." I wondered what he meant by funny—I was terrified of him.

The situation was horrible, and it wasn't safe. I hated being alone in the house, helpless as it unfolded. I wasn't prepared for any kind of struggle. I noticed his faded blue jeans were bulging; I wasn't sure what was in there, but I moved cautiously to avoid appearing unduly bothered. I sat next to him, wondering why he had come. Did he come to repent? I wasn't interested in his repentance—safety came first. The atmosphere felt like a helpless child running into a den of lions, with the biggest lion clearing the road for the goat.

He moved from his seat and came over to me. He told me he had always wanted me and would care for me until his last breath. He grabbed my left arm, but I pulled his hands away. He started touching my arm again, and I yanked them off once more. I noticed he was becoming upset. His eyes were bloodshot red, and I stood up and shouted for help as he began to unzip his pants. The noise from the living-room loudspeaker drowned out my voice. He moved closer, but I ran as fast as I could toward the stairs. As I tried to go down, I realized my gown had caught on a nail in our wooden steps. The next thing I remember was waking up in the hospital.

I became conscious and saw my mom talking furiously to a middle-aged Asian woman in a lab gown. I wasn't sure who she was, but she spoke quietly to my mom. Then I saw the doctor walk into the room. He talked about my deep injury, which could have been worse. My head was bandaged, but the pain from it was nothing compared to the pain that came from my mother's words. She spoke on the phone, saying the person should not mind me and that I wasn't normal again. She spoke as if I had carried myself from the room and crashed into the wall.

My mom picked me up from the hospital. I was surprised she wasn't too busy to get me—she arrived right on time. I was becoming agitated sitting in the room waiting. Pain layered every part of me as I sat in the back of a gold Chevy truck. She was dressed in blue jeans and a red checkered shirt.

As we drove home, she played some music, which I really didn't mind. She talked about the hardships her job was facing—losing contracts and company buildings closing. She worked so hard, yet the company did not allow its members to buy contracts or enjoy the same rights and recognition as other employees in the city. She would sometimes drive without mentioning anything or anyone and later return to explain how deep the company's troubles had become and how the world seemed to forget people who worked in the economy. She went on and on and never looked back to see if I was listening; she assumed I was.

I didn't stop her from expressing her thoughts or talking about things so dear to her heart. I couldn't dare interrupt her—she would probably start yelling. I could feel her burden. She was a mom with responsibilities, working to care for her family even when the bills piled up. She spoke about it calmly but insisted on how good life would be if those at her job, including her, had access to health insurance, social benefits, and better pay like employees at larger companies. She was obsessed with the federal government stepping up and saving nonunion workers by recognizing their labor just like regular employees in the city, with equal benefits. I knew she was pained and needed to speak her mind. Her painful complaints had been the same tune for years.

When she was mad, she was mad. Sometimes I thought she was a broken record—I could hear her in my sleep, repeating the same refrain. I would put my music on in my bedroom to drown her out, a low-volume track from MTV. Over time, I realized my shame wasn't the main thing occupying my mind; it was the pain I had carried for years in my heart. It didn't stop the awful feeling that lingered from my Uncle James after he moved out. Shame still ate at my soul as always. I had pains no one even knew about, while the world appeared the same to people who carried intense hurt.

The sound of the car tires snapped me back to reality; our driveway was right there. I knew I was home. Whether I would be welcomed back wasn't the issue. As she sped off, I thought the burden in my heart would vanish just as the music from the car faded. That assumption was wrong. I was greeted by sudden changes throughout the house.

The sofa I had placed before the unfortunate incident was gone, and the flower vase along the fireplace wasn't there anymore. It felt as if I had been away for years. But those changes at the entrance weren't the real surprise. The main surprise sat in our living room—cooling off with an iconic light bottle of beer, his favorite drink. The smell took over the room as he positioned himself on the couch. One thing that struck me was my mom's black couch with zebra pillows in the living room. Still, that wasn't the main issue.

The problem was that my uncle—the man who had violated and assaulted me for years—sat comfortably in our living room, enjoying himself while I riddled with pain and a stench of anger. His presence brought the memories back in full force. I wondered if I had lost my mind or was losing it. My head pounded; it felt like a migraine boiling inside me. I was raging and frightened; I was reliving it all intensely. The headache became a burning migraine that churned inside.

It disturbed me that the memory of my violation would continue to shadow my life even while he looked so innocent as he slept. He later told my mom he was going on a trip. I wished he would be gone forever. He would take some time before he returned. I left the living room with the last of my strength—burdened, worried, and pained by all that shame.

CHAPTER 17

I broke up with Michael, but several things played out before then. Michael had once been precious to me, and I wasn't ready to let him go. I just wished he could go back to the way he was when I first met him. Crazy, huh? I trusted that somehow things would change, but instead I was left alone. I didn't take immediate action about whether to break up with him or not. I hoped things would get back in shape. It was all a dream I was living.

I was still in the agony of the violation from my uncle, which had already begun to shatter me. Then Michael worsened the situation by throwing me out to his friends for money. I wasn't desperate—I only wanted to live. He thought he could treat me like a piece of waste, and I was never ready for that. My mind hadn't chosen a direction yet, but succumbing to despicable treatment from Michael was not an option.

I thought of what to do, but I felt sick whenever I remembered how he had endangered me at that hotel. It was upsetting that Michael hurt me—hurt me with his decision to prioritize money over me. He shoved me down and set me up to make money for himself. After my horrific encounter with the strange man he hooked me up with, I wasn't okay with him anymore. And yet, he continued. He always set me up with someone who wasn't decent. He even assaulted me right after that incident, and that complicated everything further.

All I wanted was to survive, but Michael showed me that whether I lived or not didn't matter to him. He was cool with making money; my life meant nothing to him. I was pained by his selfish, heartless attitude. I wanted to be free from every shackle and bitter experience.

Not long after the incident, he texted me saying he wanted to see me. I wasn't interested in seeing him, but deep inside I still loved him and wanted him to care for me. Still, I didn't reply when I got the text.

I was in the middle of resting. A shiny wooden stool stood before me, with a couch at the other end of the open living room. I sat on an arm-free chair with a green cup in my hand, drinking water as if I were sipping brandy. I wanted to drink so badly, but I was trying to avoid alcohol.

The memory of that ugly night flashed in my mind. I remembered how unkempt the room at the hotel was and how the man nearly forced himself on me. The strength I summoned that night was like never before. Still, I didn't feel good about any of it. My anger was directionless. I wasn't sure if I should be angry at myself, at Michael, or at life itself—life that had continued to push me from one painful end to another.

The text from Michael made me furious. I had second thoughts about replying, wondering what would come from meeting him again.

That afternoon, I hurriedly dressed. I picked out a blue top, the same shade as the sky. I had agreed to meet Michael at a spot not far from my place. I had gone to bed late the night before and had to rush to make it on time. A faint soundtrack was playing in the background as I dressed.

I thought about when I first met Michael and how intensely in love we had been. I had always believed he would be there for me. He impressed me with his charm, and back then, I was too young to understand his true intentions. I always had his back. I did everything for him. But things hadn't played out the way I thought they would.

It was Michael who had first introduced me to meeting men for money. He made it seem like help, but what sort of help was that? I knew I wasn't like this before. Even after my uncle had violated me, I hadn't planned to go down that path. I wanted to hold onto some sense of sanity. That was why, at first, I wasn't sure if I should bring Mary, my therapist, into my secret.

Michael exploited me, no doubt. But my sight was blurred by love—I couldn't see beyond the pretense he offered me as love.

I remembered trying to send him a breakup message after that night. I had already typed it: *"I gave my all to you, but you dragged my hope through the mud of life."* I was about to hit send when a thought came: forget about the whole thing. Michael, my violation, my secret—I wanted to push them all aside.

I wanted to get my life together, but it was an arduous task. You know how heavy a load can feel when you carry it alone and have no one to cheer you on—depressing would be an understatement.

I stepped into a green-checkered cab outside and settled in for the ride. The driver had switched on a recording. I wasn't sure if it was a lecture, a podcast, or an audiobook.

My attention wasn't on what the driver was playing. I was half-minded, replaying what I had just seen a few minutes before I left to meet Michael. A young man, maybe in his thirties, was continuously punching a lady. People crowded around, trying to rescue her, but as the car moved past, I could still see him dragging her to the ground.

I was moved to tears. I wanted to get out of the car to help her. I wanted to challenge him. I wanted to ask why he thought she deserved to be treated as if she were worth nothing. Why did he treat her like a punching bag?

The driver, however, paid no attention to the assault. Instead, he nodded his head to the audio that kept playing. The speaker talked about how interpersonal relationships are sustained by love languages. He listed quality time, gifts, touch, words of affirmation, and acts of service. He particularly emphasized how acts of service show value in other people. The driver just kept nodding until we reached my destination. Then I got out.

The garden was lush, green, and serene. Michael had texted me the name of the place and told me he was coming. I came purposefully, hoping to hear what he wanted to say—and why he felt he needed to explain what he had done to me.

I sat on a bench by the table and looked out through the glass building. I waited for Michael to show up. At a nearby table, a couple in their fifties laughed through their private conversation, their voices muffled, their joy spilling over. They were wining, dining, and laughing. I stayed silent.

The garden breeze moved as though it was playing with the trees, and the peace of the place made me wish for a return of bliss in my own life. I longed for change—from sorrow to freedom.

I waited the first hour, then the second. The time passed, but Michael never came. I thought maybe he didn't want to come at all, so I left.

When I got home, I met my mom. She was reading *Jet* magazine. She looked up at me and asked if I was fine, judging by how I looked. That was the first time she had looked into my eyes and asked if I was okay since the violation by my uncle. I mumbled something, then later said I was fine.

I walked to the other side of the room, feeling both heavy and light at the same time. She continued reading her magazine. Deep inside, I still hoped she would come back fully into my life—that she would be the same mother who was always with me and for me before my uncle entered the picture.

Then she spoke about her friend who had just been laid off from work. She talked confidently about her friend's innocence and how the allegations against her had been misplaced. She explained that her friend had been harassed by a male supervisor because she refused his advances. My mom was deeply moved for her friend and hoped justice would come.

But all I could think was: would she ever realize the pain caused to me by my uncle? Would she ever give me the comfort she so freely wished for her friend?

I later learned that Michael didn't show up at the spot because he had gotten himself into some trouble, though I wasn't clear on the details at the time. He had moved to another area near the hotel, engaging in things he had no business doing. Michael had approached a schoolteacher at a local high school on the west side and was supplying drugs to the school.

The principal hadn't paid much attention to the whispers that students were abusing drugs—at least not until homecoming day. That was when two students went behind the school building and tucked wrapped items into their backpacks. Nobody noticed until those students acted strangely, high and disruptive, during the homecoming party.

The matter escalated when one of them struck a teacher who had stood in his way. The teacher felt humiliated, and the incident was immediately reported to the principal. The student was called to the office but refused to appear—an insult and an affront to the staff. The principal then went classroom to classroom, calling male students out one by one. The first few denied knowing the student who had assaulted the teacher.

Realizing his approach wasn't working, the principal ordered the students back to their rooms and called for another meeting the next day. This time, he gathered the teacher who had been assaulted along with several others. Among the students stood a boy in a green shirt, close to a man in a dark navy suit. Next to him were two other boys, one of them clutching a small black bag with trembling hands.

The man in the navy suit spoke quietly with the principal, then turned to the students, pressing them to reveal who had given them the drugs. At first, they refused to respond. But after repeated questioning, one student finally admitted that a junior class teacher had supplied them. Shock rippled through the office—the principal, teachers, and staff were all stunned. To make matters worse, three junior class teachers hadn't shown up to the meeting, raising further suspicion. Eventually, the students identified the teacher by name, and the meeting was dismissed with instructions to return the next day.

Michael wasn't aware of what was happening at the school. He had continued with his prostitution scheme—supplying girls to his wealthy customers and making money off them. He had a thing for sharing girls with his rich friends to make money while appearing to live large. He was known as the dope man of Detroit.

We hadn't spoken since his last message, and he refused to show up at the building. He seemed to enjoy life so much that he didn't even care if I existed. One evening, he drove to a hotel and dropped off another girl for a client. Afterward, he lingered outside. When some girls moved around the lobby, their movement made him uncomfortable, so he stepped outside.

Outside, he noticed some men circling his car. He immediately grew cautious and stopped moving closer. He wanted to know who they were and why they were hanging near his car at that time of day. But he didn't go any further. The men eventually withdrew. The problem was that he hadn't seen their faces and wasn't sure who they were. He convinced himself he didn't have much to worry about. As long as he kept making money from the girls he linked with men at the hotel, business would continue to boom.

He went back inside, later emerged with the girl, scanned the area carefully, and then sped away.

The next day, Michael met a man in Timberland boots to pick up drugs. The packages were wrapped so thickly no one could see what was inside. He sped off after the exchange. Later, in a neighborhood, he stood near a black iron fence, tossed the drugs over, and watched another man grab the bundle and drop it into a larger bag. Michael drove off, and the teacher went his own way.

The Healing Wound

Later, the identified teacher—the music teacher—stood before the committee answering questions about his role in bringing hard drugs into the school. The students confessed they had paid for every item they received, and the teacher had handed them the wrapped packages. One of the drugs was heroin, and a student tested positive for it. A confirmed case of hard drug abuse was now on record.

The principal reported the matter to the police. The teacher was arrested, and the students were interrogated. The students were separated for questioning with police and parents present, while the teacher was pressured to reveal more information about his supplier.

A few days later, the teacher called Michael to discuss new business opportunities and additional schools to target. Michael was glad to hear it and told him he was at a different hotel that day. The teacher came alone and explained that supplying drugs to a handful of students no longer paid enough. He suggested expanding—selling heroin to other schools down the street.

Michael's car was parked between a brown Jeep and a gray-painted Monte Carlo. The teacher asked if Michael had drugs with him. Michael pulled some wraps from under his seat, then grabbed another bag from the back seat. The teacher laughed, saying he was ready for business. Michael opened the bag—it contained heroin and cocaine. The teacher laughed again and suggested they start selling in the neighborhood, not just to students.

They both began sniffing, and Michael took a syringe to inject himself with a hard liquid substance. That was when police barricaded the car and ordered Michael and the teacher to get out. They complied and were arrested on the spot.

After being caught, Michael was detained and confessed to trafficking hard drugs, even selling them to schoolchildren. The case dragged on for some time before he was sentenced to jail.

After all he had done to me—dragging me into drugs and selling my body—I was finally free from him. That chapter of my life was closed. If only I could close the chapter with my uncle as well. I longed for happiness.

CHAPTER 18

Outgrowing pain goes beyond the physical. It demands a state of deep reckoning—aligning your inner life with your outward life—to leave the past behind and move forward to a place of growth. I had been there; I had been in a place of striving, pain, and agony. It became a choice: either to stick to living in the past or to move toward beautiful moments created by self-love, self-appreciation, self-realization, and satisfaction.

I was abused by Uncle James, and that act turned my life from moments of blazing stars to a dark sky looming over everything. I was like a blooming flower cut short and left in a gory situation. I was stuck, wallowing in tears and suffering—the sorrow that accompanied my grief. It was turbulent; that encounter with Uncle James led me into a series of ugly, shapeless, soul-denigrating experiences.

My mom's handling of the issue from the outset made it larger than it was; she portrayed me not only as a terrible child but as a misfortune sent to ruin her relationship with her boyfriend Johnny and even to implicate Uncle James. Of course, my mom never believed me from the moment I was violated. I took several steps to make her see the reasons and the suffering I endured because of the violation, but she never did. She thought I wanted to bring her down, to take her from relevance into an unknown, oblivious state. That was never the case. I was in pain—the pain that followed me from my bed daily to everywhere I set my feet: from the grocery store to the walkway, the classroom, and neighborhood to neighborhood.

It reminded me of the time my therapist, whom I had trusted, let me down—an act that added salt to my injury: pain upon pain. It was a journey of dying silently. You know how a cancerous cell is eaten in stages—sometimes the victim doesn't know, or even if they do, they feel powerless to fight. Yes, that was exactly my case. My tumultuous experience of violation damaged my self-esteem, self-worth, and confidence. I thought I had ruined my family and become an outcast. Who could have thought I would experience that so early in life? I had been in that place where it hurts. But did I have to stay there forever? I wanted an answer.

If you find yourself in a pit, the next step is to call for help. I called for help by getting another therapist. It started well. You know how a beautiful love story usually starts—where a young lad finds a breathtaking damsel and would sacrifice everything for her. That was how my therapy story began. I didn't want to open up to my therapist initially, but I later did. In the process of opening up, I thought I had found solace, but I was wrong. My new therapist moved away, leaving me in feverish conditions of life. I was treated like that teenage girl who was heartbroken by the guy who would have climbed any hill to watch her smile. Like a balloon punctured from behind, so was my therapy love shattered. Would I ever want to pick up the pieces? You could ask that again.

Beyond therapy, I trusted my diary to find me healing again. I had read about monks and how they relied on natural healing, which also involved writing. Of course, I know that writing is one of the greatest discoveries in human civilization. That, however, was not my concern. I saw writing as a diagnostic process where penning my emotions could check into the veins, heart, and capillaries of life. I wanted natural medicine to flow from my diary into my life. I wanted my moments to rise from solitary pains to shared joy and exhilarating living with others. I was tired of waking up in my tears and sleeping soaked daily. I wanted a turnaround.

But you know, it was never that easy to break loose from the excruciating things of the past and define beautiful moments of life. Would there ever be any beautiful moments? I wondered if life would ever be meaningful. Yes, success would come to my life once again. I mean bliss would litter the streets of my heart. I would journey from agony to laughter, from forgotten to remembered, from a useless piece to a valuable being. That would indeed be great. I didn't find the intensely craved healing in my diary. I pierced my heart in flowing emotions and penned my disappointment to no avail. Healing didn't show—or maybe it went on a vacation.

I didn't recover from the anger stuck in my heart, the hidden, burning hatred for my Uncle James, or the relentless disrespect I nurtured toward my mom. These were what I harbored inside, and healing never came close to me. It was like moving from the frying pan into the fire. I wanted to get better, but I couldn't. The past had the best of me, and life treated me like I was worth nothing. I needed to heal from my abuse.

When the mind is sick and you visit a physician, after a thorough examination, you're recommended medication to spring back to life and recover from your ailments. That was exactly what I longed for. I wanted a prescribed dosage that would erase my past and carry me into bubbling moments with no stain of yesterday. I searched everywhere but couldn't find it.

I was affected by my past in school, in my relationships with others, and even within my family. No one trusted me, and I found it tough to trust others. My trust box had been battered to the point that I cared nothing about trusting anyone ever again. Trust meant nothing to me. After all, in my mind, all humans were selfish, callous, greedy, and manipulative.

One sunny afternoon, I was walking down my street on the Eastside of Detroit when I bumped into a middle-aged woman with not-so-blonde hair. Maybe I had an unclear mental picture of her hair.

She looked pretty, but her beauty didn't catch my attention. I had plugged in my earpiece, meditating as I walked along the less busy neighborhood road. The lyrics playing were something like, *"If you want to leave… don't leave alone… the colors are changing…"*

I was disconnected from the music, fixated on my thoughts instead. Yes, my thoughts became my jam, and instead of moving to the rhythm, I carried on a soliloquy with my escaping reflections. I guess the woman noticed me from afar and followed. I wasn't concerned about her or her movement; I was only lost in thought as I walked.

Then something tapped me back to reality. No, I wasn't hit or harmed. Rather, this woman walked past me gently, and I was entangled in the soul-lifting perfume she wore. It made me glance to the side. She turned back to look at me, and in that moment, I returned to reality.

I later learned her name was Gina. She had a Latino background but had lived in the state for a very long time. She introduced herself and asked why I walked with such detachment. I had no real answer, only a quiet thank-you for pulling me back into awareness. She then asked if we could sit somewhere and talk. Normally, I would have declined such an invite from a stranger, but I had second thoughts and said, *"Why not?"*

That was the beginning of my self-conscious journey toward healing. I wouldn't say I went searching for healing—healing came knocking and found me.

Gina told me how surviving rape and living through her own gory past led her to become first a psychologist, then a counselor. Her description of the sad life of a rape survivor stuck in the past fit perfectly with mine.

She spoke about how she was inspired by her troubled past to help women heal and live better lives. She spoke with power and captured my attention. But you know those moments when you hear things that've become weary, and you just can't find a place to hold them in your heart. Yes, Gina's message of hope was brilliant. I didn't see her as anything beyond a nice woman doing incredible things to restore hope in the world.

Yes, just like the United Nations helps troubled territories keep the peace, or helps countries respond to disease outbreaks, or like Bill Gates donating to end malaria in Africa—Gina's work seemed like that kind of charitable effort to me. I left her that day, but fate would have us reconnect two months later. This time, I had been ruminating on Gina's call to start afresh and build something beautiful. I didn't even have a block, much less an empire. Maybe it would be a story of the rejected stone becoming the chief cornerstone of a house—a daydreaming kind of thing.

I wasn't entirely wrong to think something great could come out of my Nazareth. It might not be as grand as building the next Imperial Valley or making my life as attractive as Central Park Tower, but I was surely heading somewhere—unnamed, yet known—an end with certainty where hope is restored and life would make sense again.

I started sharing my story with Gina—how I failed in my studies because I couldn't concentrate. My past held me so tight that every day seemed worse than the one before. I was often suicidal. I wanted everything to end. I didn't want the putrid smell of my life to continue contaminating everything. Was I going to commit suicide? I wasn't sure.

Since I was teetering on the brink, nobody could have predicted what I would do. One thing was sure: I was tired of everything. Maybe death would be better and more peaceful, I thought. Gina saw the misty look on my face. She had been there. She was happy I didn't give in to my deadly thoughts. She made me realize that not giving up was a victory. I won the moment I didn't commit anything drastic when my heart was suicidal. I wondered why I hadn't given in but couldn't say specifically. Maybe death would have been a bitter pill to swallow. It was a state of uncertainty, but I didn't break. Gina knew I had won when I told her what I had wanted to do. I didn't see any victory, but she saw a conqueror. Maybe she was not strong enough to admit she had won over her life, but she had.

I told Gina how I dreamed of stabbing Uncle James to death. I pictured a room filled with stench and littered with blood. In my dream I stabbed Uncle James, locked the door, and poisoned myself. I thought I had died until heavy noises filled the house, and I began to stir in blood. It was the noise, the bleeding, and the offensive smell that snapped me back to life. I wasn't dead, but I saw a lifeless body before me. I couldn't remember anything clearly. It felt as if I had lost my mind. Although memory failed me, the room seemed familiar, and I struggled to crawl toward the body lying in a pool of blood. Alas—it was Uncle James.

Should I rejoice that I had finally ousted my violator, or should I begin to think of the years of sentence I might face for murder? As I struggled with that question, I felt a rush of air across my face. I later realized I hadn't closed the window before I fell asleep—I had only been dreaming. I came back to consciousness.

My moments with Gina at first felt like the therapy sessions I'd had before. I talked over everything I had experienced, and she told me how different women had become despicable because they couldn't heal from their violations. Before I met Gina, I was in a state of worthlessness. She told me the first step to healing the heart is to know what the heart is capable of. I wanted to heal but didn't know how. Later I would realize that my desire to heal was itself a step toward victory—a motivation to heal, whether consciously or unconsciously.

My situation was like that of a man hungry for days in isolation who suddenly found himself in an unfamiliar place—he would still be hungry but unable to eat because he didn't know where to find food.

I wanted to overcome my fears, triggers, and dark memories, but it wasn't easy. Journeying with Gina helped me.

First, I knew I needed something. As it's usually said, the first step to getting what you want is to know what you want. For so long, I didn't know what I wanted, so I wandered a lonely path, unknowingly traveling toward a no-return city of sadness. But once I realized I needed to heal before anything great could emerge from my heart, I became interested in healing—and that in itself was healing.

You know, recovery comes in stages. Just like a woman convalescing from an illness, it's not something that can be rushed. The medication must settle into the right part of the body before chemical changes take place and begin motivating physical, mental, and emotional healing.

The second step came when Gina invited me to an all-girls campaign in the neighborhood to walk against sexual violence perpetrated against women and teenagers. During this campaign, I met amazing people who also helped me find both the attractiveness and the desire for healing.

We gathered at the end of the neighborhood road. At first, I didn't feel the purpose of walking around to raise awareness, but I later understood the value of the movement when women and teens began to share their experiences.

An aged woman told us how she had suffered sexual abuse as a young married woman. She despised anything connected to violation because after her encounter she nearly died. While still in her pain, she was struck down on the street by a careless driver who ignored traffic rules. She survived the accident, only to become suicidal afterward. She wanted to leave the earth badly, but eventually, light came for her at the end of the tunnel. She cherished the coming together of all ages to speak out against such despicable acts in society.

A girl in her early twenties, wearing nicely striped jeans, shared how she was ridiculed by her peers at school. Some boys she had rejected thought revenge would be the best punishment. They cornered her late one evening and violated her. Though they were later caught and punished by the school authorities, the damage had already been done. A young, innocent girl was scarred with stigma—what a cruel way to kill dreams, hopes, and futures.

Going with Gina to these campaigns gave me leverage to first understand that I was not alone in my struggles. Yes, it was a struggle. And as the Liverpool football team would say, *"You'll Never Walk Alone."* I realized that healing meant never walking alone. I knew I would need to strengthen my outward life as well as my inward life—it was that important to heal inside and out.

I appreciated Gina for introducing me to Lopez, who was devoted to writing about cases of violation. I enjoyed reading Lopez's books and articles on how terrible the violation of women, teenagers, and children had become. Whether through writing or through neighborhood campaigns, the mission was always the same: creating awareness about what people were going through and demanding change.

Those changes needed to include policies to better protect young girls, teenage women, and women in general—and to ensure abusers didn't go scot-free. Punishing violators would also serve as a deterrent to others nursing such sickening behavior.

I volunteered with the *Michigan Sexual Assault Group* as a research contributor and field officer. As a contributor, I read about cases of abuse and how people suffered. Many never got justice; some died before their cases were even heard. Only a few ever found relief.

Volunteering became like lifting the burden of life away from me. Every weekend—once the epicenter of my gloom—began to change. I was no longer staying alone in the house, drowning in tears. Now, I joined the campaign team to raise awareness about girls' empowerment. I also contributed important facts and figures for publications on policymaking, implementation, and strategies to build greater awareness of sexual violence against women and children.

Volunteering was like starting a new journey in life. It was like a planted seed shooting up from nowhere, spreading across the surface to grow strong.

Of course, it would need to be watered so it would not die. The watering was entirely another part of life. Yes, I got to love again. This time around I had already moved beyond the pain caused to me by Uncle James. I was not seeing pain anymore. Instead, I was seeing my superpower that lies in my self-responsibility, accountability, self-love, volunteering, and peacekeeping with others. I began to see I could do amazing things. My experience validated the saying that it always seems impossible until it's done. Yes, it always seems impossible, but I made it anyway. Once I realized that I could heal, there was no going back. I wanted to heal, and I healed.

You know it's like a planted rose bush that needs to be watered. Watering is mostly things happening in the environment finding their way into the mind—that is, the soil of the heart. If negativity keeps sinking into the mind, then the body would be full of negativity, and life itself would exude negativity. I understood that, and I never wanted negativity to run the affairs of my life.

Not long after, I attended a speaking contest at a church in Warren, MI, the next town over. I had gotten the invite from Lopez, who was also invited by her longtime friend. Lopez had other engagements, so she encouraged me to enter the contest. I was sore and afraid. I didn't want anything that would trigger my emotions. I knew I was not good enough; I felt worthless and like a stark failure. I was just trying to see if I could heal—why then would I leave healing to enter a contest where, if I failed, I may never recover? I didn't know that exercising the mind was healing.

I started preparing for the contest late, but I later got my points together and decided to give it a try. After all, failure may mean the beginning of something good. I was terrified onstage when I lost my thought mid-speech. I mentioned something about imposter syndrome, and then flashes of Uncle James hit me—how I had been screaming for help that day. I never expected this. I thought all would be well and I would recover fully. That was my hope. I wanted to disappear from the stage and find myself back in my room, sinking in a pool of tears over how big a failure I had become.

But then I heard a loud cheer from the audience—maybe someone read my mind or my lips—and what followed was a heavy drumbeat of hands that saved the show. I paused to let the audience cheer me on, and then I zoomed back to life. I was surprised when I emerged as the winner and received one thousand dollars as a prize. That indeed was a redefining moment for me. It changed my perspective on life.

Then I realized that I could do wonderful things in small places. Days after the contest, I received a lovely letter from Gina praising me for carrying the flag of excellence at the contest and telling me how they had rooted for me—which I had not disappointed. Lopez sent hers as well, and it was filled with love. These people cheered me on, and I felt love again.

I wanted to hear myself again, so I asked the contest organizer to send me a soft copy of my speech. I turned that speech into a daily anthem. Instead of choosing to cry, I would listen to my speech. The speech reflected the good, the bad, and the ugly, but beyond that it was phenomenal—a sign of strength, courage, and brilliance returning to a shapeless life. I found my voice again, and life was beginning to make sense.

Would it be only short-term relief? I wondered for a while, but I was ready to see the end of it all—short or long.

I met Francis at one of our girl-empowerment advocacies. He

had come as a grad student trying to learn what was happening in the community. He was researching sexual violence and assault as a doctoral student. He asked if I could help him fill out a survey for his research and introduce him to the problems faced by girls in my college, and if they might be interested in participating in the survey. I obliged. I realized he was working on something meaningful that would benefit society.

We started talking from that point. Later, he asked me out to dinner, which I refused three times. But he didn't back down. He encouraged me to give it a try, and yes—his persistence helped in a way. I wanted to be sure he wasn't just a random player out to use me and treat my heart like a bouncing ball. I enjoyed our occasional chats and eventually agreed to meet him at the hub where Gina and Lopez worked for girl advocacy.

The hub had an outdoor seating area, and we sat there talking about everything—from his perspective on studying sexual assault to what I was studying, from my favorite color to his passion for poetry, and from his love of journaling to my lost interest in it. Our conversation was interesting, and we got along quite easily.

We dated and shared moments of growth together. He got to know about my painful experience with Uncle James, and that honesty became a seal for our relationship. He never wanted more pain to touch me, and I didn't want anything harmful to befall him. Our love burned deeply—more than that of Romeo and Juliet. Although our story wasn't set on the streets of Mack Avenue, it was unique for its understanding, shared values, and consistent communication.

Francis' relationship with me placed my healing on a pedestal of smooth progress, with no return to sorrow. I glided through the process once he became a support system for me. He never let me down, and I ensured I stood with him too. Our love led to three wonderful children, even though we never married. Would you call that a love set in Jupiter or Mars? Of course not—it was set here on earth, and it lasted the test of time. That was the beauty of it all.

I healed. Healing became my anthem. It wasn't sudden, but I healed. I leaned on Gina's touch, Lopez's exposure, and Francis' steady backbone, and it felt as though I walked on eagle's wings over the storms of life. What mattered was that I healed without putting anyone else in danger.

I also realized that not getting justice in my case didn't mean other girls would never get justice or that rapists would always go scot-free. Something was kindled in me: a passion to pursue the truth and ensure that every girl, no matter where she is or what she has been through, can get justice, can heal from pain and tears, and can one day tell her story of grief and fear from a place of freedom.

I caught fire in those campaigns against sexual abuse alongside Lopez and Gina. That fire sparked a realization of the depth and breadth of excellence within me—excellence that, if allowed to the surface, could be magical in making the world better for girls. I wanted no girl to endure the trauma I had, no girl to lose love or grow up in a pain-filled home.

I thought about how best to help others without barriers, and writing about my experience rose to the top. Through writing, I could show the world what I endured, how it happened, how I survived, and how I healed. I knew this book would prove that losing hope is never the way out—that you can heal, no matter how dead the violation may have felt.

I believed telling my story would inspire other girls to step out of their shells, share their truth, and help save others from becoming victims. It could also help authorities put stronger measures in place to eradicate sexual violence, punish offenders, and protect survivors. I wanted every reader of this book to discard the lie that healing is impossible. Healing is healing, and my journey is proof of how it can be done.

Volunteering for campaigns against sexual abuse gave me the motivation to write this book. Francis extended his warm support too. Once, we visited a high school together where I spoke to students about the danger of silence in sexual abuse. Francis supported me by proofreading my speech and even joining the logistics team—he was the life of the event.

I relied on him as I moved from school to school, encouraging girls to see their worth, to know they were beautiful enough, and to realize they could do wonders. I knew I was touching lives as I traveled from one destination to another, encouraging young people to do amazing things with their voices and talents.

Francis and I later organized a debate competition at a nearby high school, with fifteen finalists. It was a beautiful moment, watching panelists grade the speakers and seeing the girls express themselves. I was moved to tears, realizing I could do something as powerful as filling a one-thousand-seat hall to the brim.

Yes, I did it, and Gina, Lopez, and Francis were right by my side. I did it, and it was a beautiful moment. The girls debated excellently, and the debate sponsors rewarded the winners generously. It soon became obvious that we could do something great from small places; I was living proof of that. That I could heal meant anyone could heal, no matter how terrible their past was. I decided to share my story and be involved in activities that benefit humanity—and girls especially.

I began to see signs of healing when I returned home to care for my mom while she was sick. I took care of her, and she could not hide whatever feelings hovered over her. I wasn't focused on that; I did what was needed of me—taking care of her—and I did it well. Attending to my mom's health was only one of the signs that I had healed. Other signs included my ability to speak publicly about my past, to write a book about it, to volunteer in campaigns against sexual abuse, and to devote my time to preaching safety for girls. All of those things meant that I had been healed.

I no longer wanted to bruise Uncle James like a serpent, nor did I wish harm on my mom for how she had treated me. Instead of replaying the pains I had suffered, I focused on the beautiful moments I had experienced since meeting Georgina (Gina), then Lopez, and Francis. They meant the world to me. Each time I spoke about my healing, I reiterated that it is possible to heal if you first decide it is worthy.

Once you decide it's worth it to heal, you're on the path. I doubted healing for a long time, but I eventually learned that healing comes from within—and once you set your mind to it, you can do it. I started by first believing I could heal, and then I healed.

I layered this book with my experience: how I suffered gross injustice and how my world crashed around me after the violation. I lost hope and thought nothing meaningful could ever come from me. I was wrong. I later became a single mother of three wonderful daughters. As part of my healing, I was also able to write a letter to my uncle, confronting and processing some of the pain I carried. And now, you will read that letter. And then there is this book—*The Healing Wound*—which I have pieced together to tell my story to the world, saying, "I healed."

A Letter of Healing

Finally, the day has come when I'm able to write you this letter. I no longer have any shame or think within myself that it was my fault for what you did to me. I remember what you did to me like it was yesterday. I was a little girl, just 7 years old, and when you moved in and began sexually abusing me. The first time you touched me was when you baby sat me while my mom was working. No one was there and you took advantage of me. I knew something was not right when you told me not to tell because it was our secret, and that you would kill me, and no one would believe me.

The Healing Wound

From that day on was the beginning of the worse days of my life. Every chance you got, you would touch me and make me touch you. I was pure. I was innocent. I was so afraid of you. You were preparing me for things that a child should not have endured. At 8 years old you took me to get ice cream. That was the first time you stuck your dirty hands inside my vagina. I was crying when we got home and it hurt. You told me to dry my tears so that no one would see me crying. You raped me anal just days later. I was in so much pain, and you knew it, but you kept doing what you wanted, telling me that I better not tell anyone. My little body felt so powerless. I could smell the liquor you were breathing all over me. All the time I wished that someone could have walked in the bathroom to catch you. You started raping me almost every day and at the age of 10 years old. That was big and special for you. You told me it was because that was the day you were gonna make me a woman. Only I wasn't a woman. I was just a child. How sick was that? My body was lifeless. I went into another world so that I couldn't feel it. I would block it out every time, crying and begging you to stop, only for you to say that it will be all over soon and that you love me. That was not love but you made me believe that it was.

You always convinced me to believe that it was right, and that I was your special niece. You controlled me while making me your sex object. You let your friend rape me on my 11th birthday while you watched. Not once, but twice. The next time, you sold me to him. You took so much away from me when I was a child. My joy and my happiness. You forced me into adult situations because you were so sick. Why me? Why did you have to take my childhood away from me? When the abuse ended at 11 years old, I was so happy to finally get my freedom. I was so happy to finally sleep at night without you coming and getting me out of my bed. Yet, I still had to deal with the flashback memories. You took my birthday and holidays away. I really hate what you did to me. You are a sick man. It's taken me years to get over you to gain strength, but I have Power now. You no longer control me. I have a voice and if I can save another child, I will. Your secret is about to be out. I'm exposing the monster of what you are. Yes, I'm saying all of this, I'm not ashamed, and I feel good about doing it.

CHAPTER 19

The essence of my book is to portray that healing from the past is possible. Although things might be hard and difficult to accept in situations where one's innocence has been violated, it's possible to heal and grow beyond it.

I come from a place of pain and anger. I know what it feels like to be hurt. I understand how painful it is to live without recognizing your pain—that is extremely hard to bear. Outgrowing my pain is the reason I now devote my time to volunteering for awareness campaigns against rape and sexual assault. I understand how heinous the act is and the urgent need to stop it. This is why I focus on helping young girls and women heal from their hurts.

I have beautiful children who make me happy. The happiness they bring reminds me of the possibility of raising a wholesome family, even if you come from a background of solitude and hatred, as I have experienced. I was welcomed with open hands by the women in the foundations I joined. They showed me what it means to love others genuinely. That genuine extension of love birthed in me a new reality: to support others, especially girls, so they no longer live in fear but learn to express their feelings, to live and breathe without pain, and to reach their highest potential.

I am fully devoted to helping women move away from the fear and bitterness that I once suffered. I want them to know that the law should protect them, and their abusers should never go scot-free. I do this by raising support for advocacy campaigns against sexual abuse and contributing to stronger policymaking and implementation for women's protection.

I know that when the soul is overwhelmed with sadness, it's difficult to spread the wings of possibility. One can easily be knocked down by the anxieties of life. Trust me, I have been there. However, the greatest tragedy is not choosing to heal. I believe in healing and in the beautiful things that come from it. You can do wonders if you look beyond your past and your sorrows and begin to see how elegant you are and the heights you can reach.

My ambition is to use my story to remind women who have suffered rape or childhood sexual abuse that their voices matter, their bodies matter, and their lives matter. By releasing this book, I am creating a pillar of support that proclaims it is possible to grow beyond anger and disappointment and to see the sun of a love-filled life rise again. Yes, the sun will rise again, like the "dry bones."

I believe in the greatness of every young woman struggling out there. I feel your pain, and I know how low you may feel. My message to you, however, is this: do not give up.

You are adorable, gorgeous, and strong—a warrior whose beautiful flower will forever shine. Beauty never fades in my eyes; it simply appears in many forms. You are ever shining, and if another part of me were planted somewhere, it would surely grow in your struggles—struggles I know will one day bloom into the next amazing story that changes the world.

Connect With the Author

Facebook
The Healing Wound

Instagram
@_marketastrongsurvivor

TikTok
@_marketastrongsurvivor

www.ingramcontent.com/pod-product-compliance
Lightning Source LLC
Chambersburg PA
CBHW071206160426
43196CB00011B/2213